THE POETRY OF
ARCHITECTURE

THE POETRY OF ARCHITECTURE

AND

Awakening Human Sensibilities to Survive Climate Change

MICHAEL N. CORBETT

with

ELIZABETH MCDERMOTT

Michael N. Corbett is a contemporary master builder who has combined the practices of architectural design and planning with construction as did the medieval master builders. He was honored by *Time* Magazine in 1999 as a "Hero for the Planet" for the design and development of the Village Homes solar community in Davis California. The first of its kind in the world, the development won widespread recognition and was visited by then-First Lady Rosalyn Carter, French President François Mitterand and other world leaders and scholars. It is still toured today, and is considered one of the best modern examples of an environmentally sensitive community. Michael was a pioneer in the sustainable design movement and lectures at universities and conferences around the world. He has served as an adjunct lecturer at the University of California, Davis and Berkeley. He is also the author of *A Better Place to Live: New Designs for Tomorrow's Communities.*

All right reserved
Published by Civil Alliance Press
Printed by Sheridan Books in the United States of America
First Edition, 2010

Library of Congress Control Number: 2010910706
ISBN 978-0-615-38713-0 (Paperback)

Assissted by Elizabeth McDermott
Foreword by Kim Stanley Robinson
Graphics and Design by Micheal J McDermott

CONTENTS

FOREWARD

When Michael Corbett, an urban planner and master builder, presented his design to the City of Davis in 1973 for a 70-acre solar-energy garden community he called Village Homes, he met with more than just skepticism. His plan was so unconventional it was illegal under several city residential codes. But three years later, after he carefully explained the reasons for incorporating a number of innovative planning and building concepts, the city council approved it against the recommendation of city staff. This major political feat was due not only to those council members who had the courage to break with the status quo, but also to Michael's persistence and commitment to his beliefs, among the most important qualities he brings to his work. Completed in 1982, Village Homes was the first community of its kind, and became a model for innovative planners all over the world, drawing such high profile visitors as President François Mitterrand of France and First Lady Rosalynn Carter.

It is this work for which Michael is most widely known, but he has continued to build and advocate for an alternative vision for development, one built around community, quality of life, and environmental sustainability. He has conveyed his message as a speaker at universities and conferences throughout the United States and Europe and as an adjunct faculty member at the University of California campuses in Davis and Berkeley. He also served Davis as a council member and mayor in his continuing campaign to help the town become a better place to live. In 1999 *Time* magazine named him a "Hero for the Planet."

Michael's work on Village Homes was part of a larger movement that had great momentum in the 1970s. At that time, the generation that came of age in the 1960s was beginning to settle down and start families, and the idealistic project of making a better world, which until then had been mostly a matter of protesting the Vietnam War and fighting for social justice, now shifted to the practical problems of living adult lives, and of creating homes and communities that matched its values. A culture of utopian design blossomed to fulfill these desires, and this culture combined the best of modern technologies with traditional wisdom. Christopher Alexander's *A Pattern Language* was an important part of this new culture, as were the Friends of the Earth anthology *Progress As If Survival Mattered*, E. F. Schumacher's Small Is Beautiful, and Amory Lovins's work on energy issues. A bookshelf or two of excellent books were published in these years, and since no one could yet foresee the coming reversals of the Reagan-Thatcher years, the hope and expectation of constructing a different way of life was widespread.

Despite this moment of hope and good theoretical work, very little changed in the realm of law—meaning building codes, zoning codes, lending requirements, and all the other small and often unnoticed laws that shape the way we build. Thus, although many communes used geodesic domes and other alternative structures, there were no complete developments built according to the new ideas—except in Davis. With the help of a small group of investors, Michael optioned 70 acres of tomato fields on the west edge of Davis. He evaluated all the ideas and concepts floating around in the progressive design community, chose the ones he liked best, added his own ideas on passive solar architecture, natural drainage and edible landscaping, and came up with a design.

After the plan was approved, Michael and his collaborators spent the next several years building. Village Homes was so distinct it was easy to spot in an aerial photo of Davis: it was the neighborhood with all the green, with narrow winding streets that looked like lanes, with bike paths, tight rows of roofs divided by gardens and orchards, and a big green communal lawn flanked by small office buildings, a community center, a pool, and a vineyard.

The "edible landscaping" that graces the village means that a large variety of fruits and nuts is part of daily life, with some of them ripening at every month of the year, providing fresh food to all and even some opportunities for communal harvesting. The village's swales, which were cut into the landscape to take rainwater to ponds, where it seeps into the groundwater rather than being swept out into the Pacific in underground storm drains, are both useful and exciting when it rains; in California, water on the land is always a beautiful surprise.

All these design features combine to have a powerful effect on daily life. My family and I have lived in Village Homes since 1991, and I can testify that the design works superbly. The built environment matters. A good design can serve as the scaffolding on which people can build a good life. Our environment shapes our habits; a communal design creates community as the default condition. Our shared ownership of this land makes us talk with each other, argue with each other, and feel a bond with each other beyond mere physical proximity.

All these elements create an effect much greater than the sum of its parts. My children have been blessed to grow up here; they don't know it, they think it is normal, but it is not. If all the American suburbs built since the 1970s had learned from Village Homes, we would surely live in a saner country and be burning a lot less carbon too.

But of course it is never too late to learn and to adapt. We will be working at this project of sustainability for a long time to come. The concepts brought to fruition in Village Homes keep coming back; they were articulated again in the 1990s, as part of "neo-traditional" town planning and the "smart growth" movements, and in aspects of bioregionalism. And now that we are in the age of climate change, the absolute necessity of de-carbonizing our civilization as quickly as possible will have impacts on every aspect of our lives, including, of course, the design of our cities and suburbs. In the twentieth century these spaces were built for cars, as if we were only the software of those more important citizens. In the twenty-first century we will be back on our feet and rethinking all that. And when it comes to rethinking town and neighborhood design, Michael Corbett has already started the process.

In this book, he has elaborated on some of his core ideas and illustrated them by including beautiful photographs taken while he traveled through Europe and studied the built landscape there. He shows us towns that are perfectly situated to their place, not just functional but lovely. They are in human scale; the people living in these towns seem comfortable, somehow at peace. The planning theory behind these places has been honed by centuries of practice and refinement, until the result is really a work of art.

Michael has looked to these places to find their poetry and their pattern language, and now he presents some of them to us as a knowledgeable guide. He analyzes the features that help to reinforce a sustainable community and that could be incorporated into the building we will be doing in the years to come. Above all he uses them as indisputable proof of how much has been lost in the beauty and artistic expression of urban design and architecture. It is not just new developments that can benefit from this kind of investigation. Poor design has reigned in the United States in the years since World War II; in many places we have built landscapes that are simply unlivable. The standard suburb creates and enforces solitude and alienation, as well as the necessity of driving to work. In this era of climate crisis, all that has to change.

So for the health of the planet and our own lives, we will be retrofitting suburbia to fit our new ideas of the good life. The automobile will be seen as a tool that got out of hand, the McMansion as a *reductio ad absurdam* of the English lord's moated castle, a questionable idea at all scales, but never more so than when shrunk to a tenth of an acre and jammed in with hundreds more. Changing all this will be a huge task, and it will take decades. An entirely different philosophy will grow into our buildings, and our patterns in space, and our habits. Throughout these decades people will be looking for models to give them ideas, and in that future Michael Corbett's work will serve as one. People will continue to come to Village Homes to see how it can be done, and now with this book Michael brings a range of such villages to you, to show you how wonderful they have been and can be again.

Kim Stanley Robinson
Village Homes resident
Author of *The Mars Trilogy*
Fifty Degrees Below
and *Galileo's Dream*

INTRODUCTION

In the late 1960s and early '70s, I was among those startled into a new reality by Rachel Carson's *Silent Spring*, Paul Ehrlich's *The Population Bomb* and Richard Curtis and Elizabeth Hogan's *Perils of the Peaceful Atom*. This awakening was intensified by the energy crisis of the '70s. We could no longer ignore the fact that we humans were damaging the environment that sustained us, or that the natural resources on which we were dangerously dependent were finite. The image of M. King Hubbert's peak oil curve, with humanity starting down the back slope, became solidly imprinted on our minds. We knew then that, at some point in the not-too-distant future, society would have to change course.

For me, this new awareness added to my concern about the ongoing destruction of the beautiful settings in which I had grown up. As a young boy in the late 1940s and early '50s, I had spent countless days in the outdoors, soaking up the beauty of the Green River, Lake Washington, and other areas in northwestern Washington. As a teenager I had spent summers in Bend, Oregon, which at the time was a small, pristine mill town on the Deschutes River. During my younger years I also visited many picturesque communities throughout California. All these places had fascinated me with the way they blended with the natural features around them—lakes, rivers, streams, forests, even agriculture. But no longer. Poorly designed, sprawling development had changed the character of all these places, and as I entered my adult years I had a keen sense of all that was being lost. I found myself increasingly compelled to try to change humanity's destructive course.

In 1973, I was able to turn my concern into action by designing and developing Village Homes, an environmentally sensitive solar community in Davis, California. But like other efforts born of the '60s and 70s' awakening, Village Homes proved less of a new beginning than a brief hiatus from the wasteful, corporate-led development model that was steadily gaining steam. Today, nearly 40 years later, corporate giants have risen to primacy, selling the general public on aesthetically clumsy architecture along with unhealthy foods, mindless entertainment, and often questionable medications, without regard for the well being of people or the environment.

It is time for a new wake-up call. With the gravity of today's global warming crisis and a deteriorating economic situation spreading across the globe, sliding downward as it tracks the back side of Hubbert's peak oil curve, we find ourselves at a crossroads. We still have a chance to restore the delicate ecological balance that makes life on earth possible and worth living, but if we choose the wrong path—the path of less resistance, the easier path—our future is certainly in peril. Unfortunately, as I look around today, people seem to be in a state of denial, confused, apathetic or angry, not knowing where or how to begin.

A journey into human history, culminating in the era just before our use of and dependency on fossil fuels started its dramatic upward climb will show us how a change in our built environment—our architecture, so intricately intertwined with the crisis we face—is an essential part of the solution. As we begin this discussion, it is important for the reader to understand that when I refer to architecture in this book, I do so in the broadest sense of the word, using it to include the whole human-built environment: buildings, their interiors and the spirit of the spaces they create; gardens and greens, plazas, bridges, towers and roadways; the layout of villages, towns and cities; and even the design and layout of crops in farmers' fields. This definition is important because all aspects of the built environment combine to make up our visual experiences, and their totality has a profound effect on the health of our planet.

Although architecture physically dominates our lives, most of us give it little thought. We rarely make the connection between good architectural design and our ability to live harmoniously with others and with nature. From the time we are born we simply accept our visual surroundings the way they are, unaware of how our mental and physical health is affected by what we see around us. We also fail to see the associations between architecture and the stability of the earth's life-supporting ecosystems, comprised of the broad spectrum of living things, the inanimate world, and the dynamics of climate.

Up until 150 years ago, because the human population was so much smaller and because building methods were so much less environmentally destructive, it was not as critical that humans understand the impacts of development. But since then, the population has exploded from slightly over 1 billion people, living in largely low-density, environmentally low-impact rural communities, to almost 7 billion people concentrated in massive, interconnected urban conglomerations supported by a high-impact infrastructure of agricultural, transportation, and energy-production and distribution systems. Under these new circumstances, it essential that human society understand architecture's effect, both on the earth and on the human psyche.

The world we have created over the past hundred years—cluttered with ugly buildings, roadside blight, billboards, and freeway interchanges, airways filled with car alarms, ringing cell phones, and revving motors, an endless stream of concocted promotional images filling our television screens and print media—has steadily eroded our ability to connect with and appreciate the beauty in the natural world and to even notice whether buildings are beautiful or ugly. Our psychological connection to our environment has weakened, and the beauty of simple pleasures—the brilliant colors and delicate patterns of clouds that can occur at sunrise and sunset, a glowing hearth, the smell of bread baking, or the sound of children playing—has been diluted by our overly complicated, frantic, machine- and computer-oriented world.

Humanity today is caught between two possible futures—one, an apocalyptic future doomed by what we have built and the way we live, and the other, a new path that lifts us to a higher level of civilization. Never before have our knowledge, technologies, and building capabilities been so powerful that they could easily provide for a future of abundance within the constraints of nature or, conversely, render the world uninhabitable by their careless and greedy use. We were warned about this paradox years ago. In *The Betrayal of the West*, written in the middle of the twentieth century when environmental threats were less dire and global warming had not yet entered the public's consciousness, philosopher Jacques Ellul observed:

> We are racing toward the end of the world and have no plan of escape, but it is considered impolite to acknowledge that fact in public.
>
> The western world is moving rapidly . . . but there is no orbit for it to take up, no point toward which it is heading, no place, no goal. We see the mistakes we have made, but we continue to make them with an apparently blind obstinacy. We know that there is an atomic threat and what it means, but like moles we go on building H-bombs and atomic energy plants. We know the implications of pollution, but we go on calmly polluting the air, the rivers, and the ocean. We know men are going mad from living in huge conglomerations, but we, like automatons, go on building them. We know the dangers of pesticides and chemical fertilizers, but we continue to use them in increasingly massive doses. We know all this, but we are like the masochist who knows others have put a little arsenic in each bowl of soup he drinks, but who goes on drinking it day after day, as though impelled by a force he cannot resist.
>
> Our speed is constantly increasing, and it does not matter whither we are going. We are caught up in the madness and hubris of the dance of death.[1]

If, in the past century, we had opened our eyes and looked thoughtfully at what was around us, we would have noticed that we were in trouble. There was a growing visual disturbance in the environment, signaling the damage we were doing to ourselves and to nature, but it was not registering in our collective consciousness. The clues were there all along. They were reflected in all that we were building, in every aspect of architecture: from city plans, buildings and landscapes to the smallest detail of our transportation and utility infrastructure. If we had been observant and thoughtful, we would have known when any part of our environment was in distress, but we were too excited by all that was new. We would have noticed that what we were creating was not visually harmonious with its surroundings, but our attention was drawn away by a growing obsession with the increasing availability of fashionable possessions. If we had been just a little bit more enlightened, we would have understood that this disharmony, this visually chaotic environment, was affecting our mental health as our recognition of beauty was being diminished.[2] Instead, we allowed imitation to replace authenticity and balance and order to fade into chaos. And this occurred at the same time we were ignorantly wreaking havoc on the natural environment. We should have realized that when nature suffered, ultimately so would we, and when our architecture became artless, standardized, and unsustainable, so would we. We failed to recognize our missteps—to feel nature's pain or even our own—and now, to our dismay, we are learning that by ignoring the consequences of our actions we have harmed ourselves, disabled the mental circuitry of society, and disrupted the self-regulating aspects of the ecosystem.

If our civilization succumbs and some future civilization discovers our remains, the most telling evidence of who we were and what went wrong would come from the ruins of our built environment. Our art and literature would tell of our beliefs, our knowledge, and our self-perceptions, but our architecture, because of the enormous investment we make in its construction and maintenance, would reflect our real values and priorities, starkly revealing them through the way we chose to live, work, and entertain ourselves and what we chose to visually surround ourselves with. So it is in architecture that we will find many of the answers to the questions of who we are, how we got here, and what path we should take into the future.

We know now that our lifestyles, intricately interwoven with technology, energy, and architecture, have caused the earth's atmosphere to revert to conditions that have not existed for hundreds of thousands of years, long before modern humans began to roam the African continent.[3] As a result, humanity is now caught in its own tangled web, woven with the fossil carbon from early life forms that was stored under the earth's surface for millions of years and is now being extracted and released into the environment at an alarming rate. This sudden spike in atmospheric carbon will continually increase with every molecule of carbon we extract, and there is no sign we are significantly slowing the process. Meanwhile, deforestation around the world, the enormous population of livestock, and melting permafrost in the Arctic are also adding massive amounts of greenhouse gases to the atmosphere. Scientists are already predicting severe consequences from the current level of greenhouse gases, with carbon dioxide in the atmosphere already 26% higher than it has been in 600,000 years, as far back in time as we have been able to date its presence from polar ice in Greenland and Antarctica.[4] Many are worried that we are approaching or have reached a catastrophic tipping point.

The earth has not always provided a suitable environment for humans. It began as a barren wasteland but was made hospitable over the millennia by the evolution of functioning ecosystems, ultimately providing the conditions necessary to support human life - food, a breathable atmosphere, drinkable water, and a survivable climate. Scientists today are unable to predict what ultimately will happen as a result of our global tampering, or if the climate will revert to conditions that cannot sustain human life. Even if we are able to physically survive in the new conditions we are creating, the rapid changes that are starting to occur may destabilize our society. If we do not act responsibly, stopping the burning of fossil carbon and preparing for the changes that have already been set in motion by restructuring our economy and architecture, it is unlikely that we will be able to avoid the breakdown of civilization as we know it.

When the unified Roman civilization collapsed in the fifth century, after years of decline with internal social problems similar to ours today—ones marked by greed, prejudice, indulgence, laziness, and corruption—much of Western society plunged into chaos. What remained bore little resemblance to the flourishing Greco-Roman culture that had dominated parts of Europe and the Mediterranean for nearly eight hundred years.[5] If our own civilization is to survive, we humans will have to dramatically change our expectations, the way we live, and the way we think about ourselves in relationship to the rest of life on this planet. We will need to undergo a revolution in thought and lifestyle. This will require a new level of civility, not only toward our fellow humans as we embrace the essence of family and community and show concern and support for all our neighbors around the world, but also toward all of nature. We will have to change our energy use, technologies, methods of food production, modes of transportation, and the design of our buildings, towns, and cities.

This is a monumental task, one that will require all the creativity and genius that has allowed humans to survive up to this point in time. Fifty thousand years ago, when a small population of modern humans spread throughout Africa and northward to populate the rest of the world,[6] it was their creativity and genius that marked them for success, helping them continually adapt to their changing environment. These early humans had a powerful intellectual capability that no other species possessed: the capacity to reason and predict events based on observation, and to communicate complex ideas; and the creativity and ingenuity to develop technologies to clothe themselves, obtain food, and build shelters. But with these capabilities and the complex expansion of the mind also came the feelings and emotions that make us fully human. Brian M. Fagan in *World Prehistory*, states:

> [These early Homo sapiens had] the capacity for symbolic and spiritual thought, concerned not only with subsistence and technology but also with the boundaries of existence and the relationships among the individual, the group, and the universe...[These were people] anatomically identical to ourselves, people with the same intellectual potential as our own.[7]

Their creative nature and ability to express themselves with symbols set them apart even from their archaic human cousins, including the Neanderthals, who could not compete in the world's rapidly changing environment and eventually died out. With their genius, creativity, and related psychological needs, our Homo sapien ancestors were able to spread around the world to survive in an astounding variety of physical and climatic conditions.[8]

Once again, humanity is at a crossroads of history. For those of us able to adapt to the dramatic changes ahead and adapt as our ancestors have in the past, the post-fossil-fuel era we are poised to enter will be a time of great challenges, opportunities, and accomplishments. But meeting the challenges and achieving success will depend on our ability to comprehend the extent of our dilemma and recognize that we are at such a crossroads. The question now is whether or not we can reach more deeply into our creative nature to bring about a change from the existing social, economic, political, and technological paradigm to a renaissance in lifestyles, business, technology, and architecture.

To tap into the full depth of our creative nature, we will have to awaken all of our sensibilities, especially our sense of beauty. By awakening our sense of beauty and allowing it to influence our decisions, we will be able to shift our approach to lifestyle and development from today's mind-set of consumption and profit at any cost to one that embodies quality rather than quantity and living harmoniously with nature.

How can something as subjective as beauty be such a powerful tool? Our sense of beauty, when attuned, provides us with the ability to feel joy and fulfillment as we form an appreciative relationship with the world around us. A sense of beauty guides our feelings about the way we interact with others and the environment and affects how we choose to live our lives, from the clothes we wear to the food we eat to the structures we choose to live in.

Reawakening our sense of beauty seems less dramatic than melting ice sheets, rising sea levels, severe storms, eroding soil, disappearing forests, and the declining diversity of our animal and plant species, yet our attention to it will prove indispensable in facilitating the larger changes in perspective and lifestyle that are needed if we are to survive. Our ability to change our behavior when needed, our creativity, our enthusiasm, and our optimism—all part of our spiritedness—are interrelated with our sense of beauty. When our ability to see and feel beauty is dampened, so too is our spirit, lowering our potential for changing our habits as well as our ability to find new solutions for the problems we face.

Ironically, in the modern race to improve our lives, we did not pay enough attention to the aesthetic quality of our built environment, allowing it to be fouled at the same time that we were fouling the earth's life-support systems. In the same way that our physical health depends on clean air to breathe and a balanced and uncontaminated food supply to nourish our bodies, so too does our mental and spiritual health depend on a sense of order and harmony in the world we see around us.

It is not that people can't survive breathing polluted air, eating contaminated and nutrient-deficient diets, and living in an atmosphere marked by visual disarray, but at what cost to our well-being and life potential? Like the degradation of our life-supporting ecological systems, which we ignored at our peril for so long, the deterioration of the beauty of our surroundings slipped by largely unnoticed. Even if the problems associated with visual disharmony are now brought to people's attention, most of us would have difficulty understanding their true scope. This can change for those willing to take the time to compare how our visual environment looks and feels today with how it looked and felt 150 years ago, before our industrial society significantly changed it.

Later in this book, we will take a journey back in time to get an idea of just how far we have gone astray. We will see that most of the detrimental changes to our visual environment happened simultaneously with our damaging assaults on nature, both occurring as humanity has become overwhelmed by the speed of industrialization. We have simply been unable to adequately understand the complex interrelationship of architecture, technology, lifestyles, the environment, and the energy we produce and use. As we have begun to look at these interrelationships, we have found that architecture affects not only the very structure and nature of the family, the community, and the human psyche, but also our environment—climatically, biologically, and, of course, visually.

In pursuing this approach, relating aesthetics and environmental stewardship, I have chosen "the poetry of architecture" as a metaphor for what once existed and what we need to regain: a harmonious balance between architecture, nature, and humanity, and the visual aesthetics that embody that state of being. The phrase was first used by English writer and philosopher John Ruskin more than 150 years ago, when that balance could be found in the intricacies of building design, from the spirit of place and space that buildings helped create, to the greens, plazas, streets, bridges, towers, and even the layout of agricultural fields. In the pages that follow I have included examples of what architecture looked like during Ruskin's era to show how architecture traditionally provided not only the means for local self-reliance and a full range of healthy social interactions, but also a consistent display of beauty, all within the limits of a hospitable planetary ecosystem.

I chose the title of this book with great humility; it is the same title used by Ruskin for a collection of articles that was serialized in J. C. Loudon's *The Architecture Magazine* in the 1830s. Still in his twenties and writing under the nom de plume Kata Phusin (Greek for "according to nature"), Ruskin subtitled the series "The Architecture of the Nations of Europe Considered in its Association with Natural Scenery and National Character." In 1893 these articles were published in a book titled *The Poetry of Architecture*.[9]

Ruskin's poetic descriptions of cottages and villas, their details, their varying styles, and the way they related to their surroundings revealed a highly romantic and compelling philosophy of architecture. He believed that we experience beauty through our feelings and emotions, and that we are affected by more than just good proportion and composition. He believed that a deeper beauty also lay in experiencing individual and cultural expression and a harmonious relationship between architecture and nature.

Ruskin was writing during one of the great turning points in human history, when several significant changes were beginning to occur. The first was the declining quality of the visual environment, as nature was being heavily exploited for resources to fuel the Industrial Revolution and gloomy industrial architecture was being built. The second was that artistic expression in the arts, product design and architecture was, in many instances, giving way to cheap replication. The third was the shift to coal and ultimately other fossils fuels as the energy used to power buildings, transportation, and industrial processes, energy that had previously been derived from the sun, wind, water, wood fuels, and animals, sources that set a natural limit on the environmental impact of human activities. Before Ruskin's time, and dating back to the Romans, coal had only been used in small quantities.

The scope and design of architecture in pre-industrial society, the low densities of the human population, and the way people lived fostered a relationship between human beings and the natural world that was generally compatible with the earth's ecological systems. Before the Industrial Revolution, societies that evolved and continued to exist in balance with nature generally lasted for centuries. When they became out of balance from deforestation, unsustainable agriculture or inability to adapt to changing weather patterns, they collapsed or declined, as was the case with the ancient Sumerians in Mesopotamia, the Mayans in the jungles of Central America, some Pacific Island societies, and the Norse of Greenland.[10] But these ecological collapses were local, not global, as is the case today.

It is in some ways ironic that Ruskin's life coincided with this critical juncture in human history, a period of monumental changes, when fossil fuels were beginning to serve as our major energy source, scientific discovery was spawning new technologies, and corporations were beginning to strengthen their influence on politics that would ultimately lead to their monopolization of the business world. As a result, decisions with far-reaching implications for the health of humanity and of earth's life-support systems were increasingly being put into the hands of these powerful economic interests, which were unprecedented in their size and scope. Up until that time values and ethics in the business world had been balanced by pride of workmanship, self-respect, and instances of altruism on one side and by the weight of greed on the other. As corporations emerged, greed became even more problematic in business operations, because corporations as entities have no conscience or sense of moral obligation. They simply exist with one motive and ethic, and that is to maximize profit. It is not surprising that at this juncture there began to be a gradual decline in the concern about the beauty of all that we were building and environmental degradation rapidly increased.

People's values and attitudes also started to change then, as life was made easier in many ways by the benefits derived from new technologies, corporate development, and industrial expansion fueled by cheap energy. But this new era also brought with it a growing list of dehumanizing changes. The world's move toward a highly centralized system of business and government, created a culture in which our reliance on ourselves, local businesses, our community, and our local resources was transformed into a growing dependence on large centralized systems to fulfill nearly all our needs. In the twentieth century, expressing ourselves artistically, entertaining ourselves creatively, interacting with our families and neighbors, and spending time in nature, where reflection and meditative thought are more easily accessible—all once a part of people's daily routine—were giving way to the activities provided by corporate-sponsored consumerism, luring us to purchase excesses of ready-made goods, foods, gadgets, and entertainment. Today it seems as though if we aren't engaged with these often unhealthy products, many of questionable usefulness, we think only to turn to the TV, computer, or mobile communication device, which, despite their many benefits, provide another endless stream of overwhelming, mind-dulling entertainment. Time spent in activities that require logical thought, ingenuity, and artistic creativity have far too often given way to the couch mentality, as we accept effortless and mindless fixes for our boredom.

With humanity having been drawn away from the social and physical environments we have genetically adapted to over thousands of years, we are now trapped in a mental fog, a hypnotic mindset induced by twentieth-century industrial society that changed so quickly that there has been no time for a healthy human culture to emerge. In fact, we seem to be held in place by the momentum of this mind-set, unable to escape its magnetic pull. Even though we are beginning to see its life-threatening failures, we are still not awake to the fact that we are now at the point, as the Romans once were, where we must change in order to survive.

To awaken ourselves to an understanding of who we are and what our real needs are as humans, we need to look to the past—prehistoric, ancient, and the time just before modern technologies, fossil fuel use, and corporate consumerism so dramatically accelerated cultural change. This will show us that culture is always evolving, as it must do now, and that we need to embrace that process so we can create lifestyles and architecture that are more compatible with nature and more capable of satisfying our basic needs—socially, physically, and aesthetically.

In chapter 1, we will discuss the dilemma caused by the failure of our twentieth-century architecture and the psychological burdens created by our consumer-driven society. We will look at what we have lost in our ability to creatively express ourselves in the face of a life based on mass production, as well as how our feelings and emotions can and should connect us to the natural and man-made environment. We will briefly discuss a subject that should be a basic part of contemporary education so that we can revive our aesthetic sensibilities: the aspects of beauty found in good proportion and symbolism. In chapter 2, we will peel back the layers of time, looking at a brief history of architectural and artistic expression in Europe to get an understanding of its evolution and how it is a part of our natural behavior.

Ruskin inspired in me the desire to see firsthand as much as I could of the beauty that he saw, to understand how the builders created their masterpieces and how the composite of all these masterpieces—the houses, the buildings, their interiors, the greens, the plazas, the streets, the roads, the bridges, the landscaping, and the agricultural fields—produced endless varieties of compositions of scenic beauty. In chapter 3, we will take a journey to experience what existed in the mid-1800s. This journey is not for the sake of nostalgia. Rather, it is intended to help us escape the bounds of twentieth-century thought and chaotic visual imageries that have us set on a deadly course. By peering into the past through the camera lens, viewing scenes of nineteenth-century architecture, we can see how people survived and flourished for centuries, in the presence of natural and architectural beauty and how magnificently varied its cultural expression was. By contrasting life now and life before our addiction to fossil fuels, we can help prepare ourselves for a changing world that will and must differ sharply from the one we live in today. This will show us how beauty and diversity in architecture can return if design once again is put in the hands of local artists who respect the local geography and culture.

In chapter 4, I will reflect on what can be drawn from our history and from pre-industrial European towns and villages that can help us find ways to restore the delicate ecological balance that supports life as we know it, so our children, and our grandchildren can survive and flourish in the post-fossil-fuel future. This will include a discussion touching on politics, economics, and education, and the efforts we must make in our personal lives, our communities, and our political system. Understanding the complicated interplay of all of these is necessary to transform our built environment, the architecture around us, so we can restore the delicate ecological balance that supports life as we know it.

My focus on Europe for inspiration is not meant to imply that beautiful architecture that once functioned in equilibrium with the environment did not exist elsewhere. Pristine villages and towns with a poetry of architecture, such as the delicate beauty of traditional Japanese houses and villages, existed with wonderful variations in every culture throughout the world. Rather, I focus on Europe because of its relationship to the work and writing of John Ruskin, its role in the development of Western society, and the limits on my time for travel. Nor do I wish to imply that the poetry of all architecture ended in the nineteenth century. Many beautiful structures in various styles were built during and after the 1800s, and architects such as Frank Lloyd Wright display an aesthetic of proportion and composition that rivals that of any throughout history, providing us with countless treasures worthy of our admiration. We are fortunate, too, that there are many architects today working at the community scale, such as Andrés Duany and Victor Dover, to mention two that come to mind, who are dedicated to reversing the twentieth-century trend of urban sprawl, drawing from the best examples of traditional architecture as they proceed to weave the poetry of architecture back into the fabric of our communities.

It is clear, however, that the sum total of the architecture of the past hundred years is not viable—environmentally, economically, or aesthetically—and that it overshadows the good work that occasionally appears like a solitary island in a sea of blight. Ruskin's ideas are a timely reminder of what we have lost—emotionally, aesthetically, and spiritually—in our exuberant drive toward material prosperity under the influence of the corporate world. Ruskin warned about this threat in his writing on aesthetics and social issues, which extended from the 1830s through the remainder of that century. Midway through his life, he began to focus more on the detrimental changes occurring in the workplace and insults to the environment. He was also concerned about the loss of genuine artistry in products and architecture. His views on aesthetics and social problems made him a critic of many aspects of industrialization, mass production, and the expanding corporate empires.

Ruskin's ideas inspired men such as Henry David Thoreau and Mahatma Gandhi, both of whom continued his example of challenging the forces of runaway greed and materialism and seeking to enlighten others. Gandhi said that another of Ruskin's books, *Unto This Last*, "marked the turning point in my life. . . . I discovered some of my deepest convictions reflecting in this great book of Ruskin's and that is why it so captured me and made me transform my life. A poet is one who can call forth the good latent in the human breast."[11] As it did for Gandhi, reading Ruskin—in my case, *The Poetry of Architecture*—marked a turning point in my life. The book became an inspiration in college, helping me solidify my design philosophy and enhancing the ideas I had already developed from courses I had taken in psychology and anthropology and from my deep feelings for nature. It brought me to the realization that good architectural design comes from considering the circular relationship of humans, architecture, and the natural world, requiring an understanding of how architecture affects human feelings and emotions and the health of the environment. Ruskin's *The Poetry of Architecture* has remained an inspiration throughout my life. His reverence for nature and picturesque descriptions of architecture heavily influenced my work as the master builder of two environmentally innovative solar developments in Davis, California: Village Homes, built in the 1970s, and Shepherds Close, completed in 2008. Ruskin's work has once again inspired me in the writing of this book. It is with a debt of gratitude to Ruskin for his inspiration, his keen sensibilities, and his insightful spirit that I offer this book, *The Poetry of Architecture and Awakening Human sensibilities to Survive Climate Change.*

CONISTON HALL - DRAWING BY JOHN RUSKIN

CHAPTER I

PRELUDE

THE ENERGY ADDICTION DILEMMA

The way we live today is both dictated by and dependent on the massive urban conglomerations we have built over the last century. We are bound to their energy-demanding buildings, industrial processes, and automobile-oriented transportation system, all of which depend precariously on fossil fuels. Our addiction to those fuels is shaking the very foundation on which Western economies are built and, as we now know, pushing the world's climate toward a tipping point that could make our planet uninhabitable in the not-too-distant future.

The environmental incompatibility of what we have built during the "era of fossil fuels" and the visual disharmony it has created reveals the sad and undeniable truth that we have lost the poetry of architecture. As noted in the Introduction, this phrase was first used by English writer-philosopher John Ruskin in the 1830s. Ruskin was writing just as the Industrial Revolution was building steam, and he foresaw the wholesale destruction of a way of life (and of building) that had existed in Europe for hundreds of years, and whose consequences we are only now coming to terms with. What remains today of the beautiful places that stand in harmony with nature—truly possessing a poetry—is overshadowed by unsustainable high-density mega-cities, sprawling residential developments, strip malls, endless commercial streets, and poorly designed buildings that have created an atmosphere of oppressive visual blight. Even well designed modern structures often lose much of their beauty in the jarring visual disarray of what surrounds them.

The most far-reaching and detrimental changes in the way we have built started at the beginning of the twentieth century, just after Ruskin's death, when the automobile began replacing other forms of transportation. Up to that point human settlements had always provided work and entertainment—as well as almost everything else people needed daily—from within or close by. The size of our communities was limited by manageable walking distances. This occurred simply out of convenience and necessity, creating the basic building blocks of human settlements, hamlets, villages, and small towns. As towns grew larger or became cities, the same constraint of convenience produced a pattern of walkable villages within the larger urban areas. Because the village form has always been the basic building block of human settlements, it has also been the center of social activities and has provided an identity for its inhabitants.

The introduction of the automobile began a process that led to the partial breakdown of existing villages. It also led to a different model for new development based more on a random pattern of dispersed activities in and outside towns and cities. In designing without the traditional constraints of walkability, city planners isolated just about every kind of social and economic activity through zoning controls. This eliminated many types of small businesses that were neighborhood or home-based. The predominant belief was that we would be better off separating our homes from our places of work, commerce, civic activities, and entertainment, segregating each to its restricted space. At that point, accommodating the automobile became a primary constraint on design. This kind of planning has been the norm in the United States and in many other places around the developed world for the past seventy years. It has created an addiction to fossil fuels by requiring that we drive to almost every activity we engage in, and we then find ourselves frustrated by being stuck in slow-moving traffic with nothing to look at but the spoiled views around us. Only in the past few decades have we begun to acknowledge how the resulting urban form, designed more for the automobile than for people, is an energy drain and is nothing less than an evolutionary dead-end for architecture.

The loss of our aesthetic and social sensibilities

As we have reached this dead end, we have also noticed that auto-oriented architecture inhibited healthy community interaction because it stopped providing the kinds of public spaces that had traditionally fostered it. Just as dehumanizing and demoralizing are the dismal aesthetic consequences of our twentieth century building splurge. What we are handing down to our children are houses, towns, and cities whose designs are incompatible with our environmental life-support systems and social and aesthetic needs. How can we expect our children to develop a healthy and mutually sustainable relationship with nature when we, their parents and grandparents, have failed so miserably at living within its limits? If the aesthetically impoverished environment we have created saddens the spirit and dulls the senses, how will our children ever know what they are missing, and how will they understand what is needed to fix it?

In his book *The Architecture of Happiness*, published in 2006, Alain de Botton argues:

> Our sensitivity to our surroundings may be traced back to a troubling feature of human psychology: to the way we harbour within us many different selves, not all of which feel equally like "us," so much so that in certain moods, we can complain of having come adrift from what we judge to be our true selves.
>
> Unfortunately, the self we miss at such moments, the elusively authentic, creative and spontaneous side of our character, is not ours to summon at will. Our access to it is, to a humbling extent, determined by the places we happen to be in, by the colour of the bricks, the height of the ceilings and the layout of the streets. In a hotel room strangled by three motorways, or in a waste land of run-down tower blocks, our optimism and sense of purpose are liable to drain away, like water from a punctured container. We may start to forget that we ever had ambitions or reasons to feel spirited or hopeful.[1]

One does not have to look far to find the visual blight that alienates us from our environment and dampens our spirit. Almost everywhere we look—in our neighborhoods, towns, and cities, and along our highways—we are exposed to architectural clutter that if it weren't ignored could only be seen as ugly. If it were translated into noise it would be deafening. Signs and billboards of every size, shape, and color invade the scenery in and around our towns and cities. As we move through our urban areas, almost every view is infected with unsightly telephone poles, towers, and wires, along with fences, barricades, enclosures, and utility structures. We are inundated with the sight of buildings of every conceivable design and material, sitting side-by-side with no sense of continuity or a logical local theme. Furthermore, most buildings, especially those in the massive subdivisions of corporate-built houses and their surrounding shopping strips and malls, are dreadfully lacking in good proportion or symbolic honesty in their details or use of materials. Their designers seem to select from a smorgasbord of meaningless detail and random materials that is then awkwardly applied without regard for local climate, geology, biology, culture, or history. The results are bizarre images of imitation materials, meaningless color selections, and odd shapes—at best an experience like a bad dream that we just get used to. Landscapes, too, are often a hodgepodge of ill-placed plants poorly suited to their locations. What we are forced to look at so much of the time—and are subconsciously trying to tune out—is an uncoordinated collection of projects, most of them designed and placed as if each were in its own small universe. Each is built without regard to how it may appear or feel to those who see and experience it, let alone to those who inhabit or work within it.

Our visual environment has been degraded gradually so that most people are not even aware of how much more pleasing and comfortable it could be. They simply do not know what they are missing. In fact, people today accept the environment they have grown up with as the norm. They have no awareness that what they have been subjected to may very well have dulled their sensitivity to beauty, restricting the lens through which they view the world, making beauty even more difficult to see and feel when it is truly there—a real loss to their potential.

This visual disarray takes its toll on us both mentally and physically. When Ruskin argued that beauty is experienced as feelings and emotions, the science of brain chemistry had not yet revealed that his assertion was correct. We now know that the experience of pleasure, whether from food, sex, companionship, personal accomplishment, music, or pleasant visual stimulation, is associated with the body's production of the chemicals dopamine and those referred to as endorphins. Often called the pleasure chemicals, they play an important role in mental and physical health. The visual environment, when ordered and harmonic, provides an important part of the pleasure stimulus that makes us healthy.

In contrast, when the visual environment is incongruent, illogical, or abnormal, it produces a stress response similar to a flight-or-fight reaction. This emotion is associated with the body's production of cortisol, the stress chemical that is useful in crises but under prolonged production builds up in the body with negative health consequences. This process occurs when we are continuously exposed to threatening social situations or to ongoing uncomfortable noise or visual experiences. In other words, what we see around us has a considerable impact on our health.

Some of us are fortunate enough to be surrounded by beauty in our homes and neighborhoods and to have access to unspoiled natural settings. But these places are overshadowed by the harsh and chaotic visual environments that make up the majority of modern-day urbanisation—devoid of the basic ingredients of beauty. The stresses created by continual exposure to disharmony and clutter may account for some of the increased anxiety, hyperactivity, and depression we see in the population today.[2]

It need not be this way. It was not so in earlier days, not, at least, until the large factories and tenement apartments began to emerge out of the Industrial Revolution. The visual environment that we have created since then stands in sharp contrast to what came before, when from every vantage point, there was a recognizable order and harmony that created a sense of beauty. Even if buildings were old and weathered and the areas around them untidy, they had a pleasing scale and proportion and created an appealing picturesque scene that possessed a logical order. Builders and craftsmen of the past were truly artisans; they were consistently thoughtful about designing and placing architecture to be beautiful and in harmony with its surroundings because that was paramount to any other constraint on them. People of that time, too, appear to have been more artful in placing objects within and around buildings, reflecting an attention to detail and style that permeated everything from personal attire to their selection of worldly possessions.

One hundred and fifty years ago, when Ruskin wrote in *The Seven Lamps of Architecture* that "architecture is the art which so disposes and adorns the edifices raised by man, for whatsoever uses, that the sight of them may contribute to his mental health, power, and pleasure,"[3] he provided insight that can help us understand what we have lost since then and can help us write a new poetry of architecture. The source of Ruskin's inspiration was, of course, the beauty of architecture before the era of fossil fuels—the beauty found in the houses and buildings and their interiors; in streets, roads, plazas, and bridges; in greens and landscaping and agricultural fields—all truly the substance of architecture.

In Ruskin's time, when people were at the market or slowly moving by foot or coach through villages, towns, and cities, it was a rich experience—observing the sensuous textures of the festive spaces or the scenic views of buildings and nature animated either by human activity or by their own movement through them. Today we move so quickly by automobile, we hardly see and feel what is around us. The time people once spent in meditative reflection—in viewing the countryside from the edge of town or looking from their windows at beautiful scenery in every direction—has given way today to a frantic rush to get somewhere, or to hours in front of the television or computer screen or on the cell phone. Most of us simply do not live in an environment that allows us to develop our individual artistic potential or to sustain a healthy emotional connection to our surroundings.

In *Beast or Angel*, published in 1974, René Dubos commented on this disconnection that so affects the human psyche:

> Social contacts may have been more satisfying by the fire in a Stone Age cave or on a village bench than they are now through the convenience of telephone conversations and of other means of mass communication. Dancing to the sound of drums in the savanna or to a fiddler on the village green

could be as exciting as dancing to electronic music. . . . The fundamental satisfactions and passions of humankind are thus still much as they were before the advent of the automobile, of the airplane, and of the television set; before the era of steam and electric power; and even before our ancestors had abandoned hunting for agriculture and for industry and had moved from the cave to the village or the city. In many cases, furthermore, modern life has rather impoverished the methods by which fundamental urges can be expressed. Modern societies can escape from boredom only by direct sensory experiences of primitive life; the need for these experiences persists in the modern world for the simple reason that it is indelibly inscribed in the genetic code of the human species.[4]

If our visual environment does not resonate with our basic aesthetic sensibilities, we are left feeling alienated and disconnected from what is around us. When it does, we are able to experience our sense of beauty and feel appreciation, admiration, and love for the natural environment and for what we have created—our architecture. This critical interaction between us and our surroundings fosters a healthy symbiotic relationship with both nature and architecture. Each provides what we need, and in return, we act to protect nature and create beauty in our architecture. I believe that hope for humanity lies with those of us who have and maintain the freedom of spirit and keenness of sensitivity to feel and understand this relationship.

Unfortunately, many who have been responsible for design and construction during the past seventy years or so have not possessed this sensitivity, perhaps because the world we inhabit has become too complex, stifling our ability to be in touch with basic human needs. Or perhaps those involved in the business of design and construction have been too naive or have succumbed to a business ethic dominated by shallow self-interest and the profit motive. Or maybe it is because change has accelerated to the point where there has been no time to evaluate the ultimate effects of our efforts. Back in the 1800s Ruskin duly noted the beginning of this trend of destructive, fast-paced development. He observed and documented how scenic beauty was being erased by ugly creations superimposed on the pristine natural setting of villages, towns and cities. In *The Stones of Venice*, Ruskin wrote of his concerns about the effects on Venice's character of modernization in general and of the new rail lines in particular:

> Although the last few eventful years, fraught with change to the face of the whole earth, have been more fatal in their influence on Venice than the five hundred that preceded them; though the noble landscape of approach to her can now be seen no more, or seen only by a glance, as the engine slackens its rushing on the iron line; and though many of her palaces are for ever defaced, and many in desecrated ruins, there is still so much of magic in her aspect, that the hurried traveler . . . may still be led . . . to shut his eyes to the depth of her desolation.[5]

At that time the world was becoming increasingly complicated, and human assaults on nature and a disregard for the preservation of scenic beauty were increasing. Ruskin's alarm is evident in a passage he wrote as he tried to record the past by drawing buildings and scenery that were slated for removal and would soon disappear as a result of new development: "I am perpetually torn to bits by conflicting demands upon me, for everything architectural is tumbling to pieces, and everything artistical fading away & I want to draw all the houses and study all the pictures, & I just can't."

He went on to lament, "Why wasn't I born fifty years ago[?]. . . . I should have saved much, & seen more, & left the world something like faithful reports of the things that have been—but it is too late now."[6]

Ruskin's world was being swept along by an irresistible new momentum. Science and new technologies were providing the means for mass production of clothing, art replicas, and building components, while fossil fuels were beginning to supply the energy for industrial processes. Architects feeling these influences were becoming more absorbed with new engineering techniques and new building materials such as cast iron and larger panes of glass. The romantic architect relying on sensuality, intuition , feelings and emotions, was becoming more of an architect of ideas, concepts and innovation. The metaphysician and philosopher within the architect were being eclipsed by the scientist and entrepreneur. More emphasis on cost and efficiencies and less on art produced a new austere industrial architecture.

Reflecting on those who would be designing the world around us, Ruskin wrote:

> [Architecture] is not merely a science of the rule and compass, it does not consist only in the observation of just rule, or of fair proportion: it is, or ought to be, a science of feeling more than of rule, a ministry to the mind, more than to the eye. If we consider how much less the beauty and majesty of a building depend upon its pleasing certain prejudices of the eye, than upon its rousing certain trains of meditation in the mind, it will show in a moment how many intricate questions of feeling are involved in the raising of an edifice; it will convince us of the truth of a proposition, which might at first have appeared startling, that no man can be an architect, who is not a metaphysician.[7]

In terms of its visual appeal, function, and compatibility with its surroundings, architecture reached its highest level of beauty when those who provided the wealth to build relied on architects, master builders and craftsmen who were thoroughly trained in the discipline of design and had advanced in their profession by virtue of their talent. Not only were these people highly capable of the masterly use of proportion within a composition, but they also understood—whether from a thoughtful analysis or intuition—the emotional effects produced by their selection of sites, orientation, shapes, colors, ornamentation, materials, and building techniques. They truly possessed a metaphysical talent that transcended what one can acquire solely from science. Science is certainly indispensible for understanding the world around us, but make no mistake — feelings, emotions and intuition cannot be replaced in the process of creating beauty in art and architecture.

Unfortunately, by the mid-twentieth century, those who displayed such capabilities had diminished in number and were often ignored. The highly evolved architects and artisans of the pre-industrial era who were responsible for the marvelous design and detail that had occurred through the ages had largely given way to a new wave of engineers, contractors and developers untrained in aesthetics and to architects who had been trained with new priorities.

By 1910 a philosophical and cultural shift was well under way in the developed world that reflected a so-called modern style, one that discounted human nature and the romantic view of artistic expression within art and architecture. In his book *The Blank Slate: The Modern Denial of Human Nature*, published in 2002, evolutionary psychologist Steven Pinker criticizes this change and refutes the beliefs of the "behaviorist" social scientists that humans do not have significant predisposition for any of their behavior, including appreciation of beauty and art, but rather start out with a blank slate, in which there is no universal appeal and all behavior is acquired or learned:

> Modernism certainly proceeded as if human nature had changed. All the tricks that artists had used for millennia to please the human palate were cast aside. In painting, realistic depiction gave way to freakish distortions of shape and color and then to abstract grids, shapes, dribbles, splashes . . . . In architecture, ornamentation, human scale, garden space, and traditional craftsmanship went out the window (or would have if the windows could have been opened), and buildings were "machines for living" made of industrial materials in boxy shapes. Modernist architecture culminated both in the glass-and-steel towers of multinational corporations and in the dreary high-rises of American housing projects, postwar British council flats, and Soviet apartment blocks.[8]

In the 1970s modernism gave way to postmodernism. Pinker describes the results:

> In postmodernist architecture, materials and details from different kinds of buildings and historical periods are thrown together in incongruous ways, such as an awning made of chain-link fencing in a fancy shopping mall or Corinthian columns holding up nothing on the top of a sleek skyscraper. . .
>
> Once we recognize what modernism and postmodernism have done to the elite arts and humanities, the reasons for their decline and fall become all too obvious. The movements are based on a false theory of human psychology, the Blank Slate. . . .

Modernism and postmodernism cling to a theory of perception that was rejected long ago: that the sense organs present the brain with a tableau of raw colors and sounds and that everything else in perceptual experience is a learned social construction. . . .

The visual system, moreover, does not drug us into a hallucinatory fantasy disconnected from the real world. It evolved to feed us information about the consequential things out there, like rocks, cliffs, animals, and other people and their intentions. . . .

Nor does innate organization stop at apprehending the physical structure of the world. It also colors our visual experience with universal emotions and aesthetic pleasures.[9]

Pinker's vivid critique of modernism and postmodernism does not mean that all of the architecture from this period is without merit. In its ideal form, the modern movement employed great proportion and composition and conveyed efficiency and harmony with nature through its simplicity of design and materials. But the building styles it spawned—spare, windowless big-box stores; nondescript tract housing; bland, uniform strip malls, to name a few—bore little resemblance to this ideal. The result was an architecture of brutalism, awkward proportion, and shock effect, clumsy architecture that lacked the qualities of beauty.

Pinker concedes, "To be fair, modernism comprises many styles and artists, and not all of them rejected beauty and other human sensibilities. At its best, modernist design perfected a visual elegance and an aesthetic of form-following-function that were welcome alternatives to Victorian bric-a-brac and ostentatious displays of wealth."[10]

The modern movement did not completely dominate architectural styles, either. Until the 1930s, art nouveau and art deco provided a more appealing and sensual approach using both good proportion and composition and a wide array of notable symbols.

Restoring our Artistic Nature and Sense of Beauty

It is these two elements—symbolism and proportion—that are integral to our perception of beauty. Their masterly use requires a special sensitivity, understanding, and talent, as expressed in Ruskin's statement that "No man can be an architect who is not a metaphysician."[11] The subjective nature of the way an artist uses them and how they affect our sense of beauty explains Ruskin's reference to a metaphysician.

Symbols

With respect to symbols, from the beginning of our existence we humans have relied on symbols to communicate with one another and interpret and navigate the world around us. When symbols are misleading, illogical, or absent from within our built environment, as they so often are today, they contribute to disorientation and confusion, and become the antithesis of beauty.

In their most basic form, symbols appear as letters of the alphabet, numbers, words and musical and scientific signs representing sounds, quantities, relationships between things, objects, actions and so on. New symbols are constantly coming into being as any graphic or object takes on symbolic meaning. Symbols can indicate ownership, status, religion and other affiliations. They can inspire or comfort. They can evoke almost any emotion. The emotions they elicit can be culturally specific, as when an icon like the Statue of Liberty—representing the ideals of freedom, justice, and liberty—is seen by highly patriotic Americans, or it can be a more intimate and private experience among a small group or even within an individual, such as when a stone carver carves a secret tiny figure, possibly a family signature, on a stone in a remote corner of a building. Symbols also play an important role in our personal artistic expression. We may intentionally use them to convey ideas and information about ourselves, or unintentionally reveal information about ourselves through our individual style and the objects with which we surround ourselves.

The embellishment on buildings as well as shapes, colors, materials, patterns and spatial relationships of buildings and landscape can be used as symbols to create emotional responses in viewers. Different elements of nature can be symbolized in architecture, for example, evoking a response based on predispositions from centuries of human evolution. The sight of a meadow, of the forest edge, of a deep and dark forest; of streams, lakes, seashores, mountain ranges; of flowering trees, cloud formations, sunsets and sunrises, the moon and stars; all of these resonate within us in a special way. We experience a range of feelings, usually positive, when we see their symbolic representation in architecture and design. Ruskin recognized these subtle connections. In *The Seven Lamps of Architecture*, he wrote:

> The Romanesque arch is beautiful as an abstract line. Its type is always before us in that of the apparent vault of heaven, and horizon of the earth. The cylindrical pillar is always beautiful, for God has so molded the stem of every tree that is pleasant to the eyes. The pointed arch is beautiful; it is the termination of every leaf that shakes in summer wind, and its most fortunate associations are directly borrowed from the trefoiled grass of the field, or from the stars of its flowers.[12]

We also respond emotionally to some abstract patterns that affect something deep in our subconscious. This kind of response evolved as we became adept at recognizing important things in our environment—dangers or food sources, for example—that increased our chances of survival. For many, a splash of warm color in a field of green brings excitement. Perhaps that emotion comes from our innate attraction to food, in this case the sight of a ripe fruit or berry at a distance. These experiences are of a symbolic nature.

Proportion and Composition

The second element integral to our perception of beauty, which resonates deep within us, is good proportion and composition. Many artists and philosophers have theorized that the most appealing geometric shapes closely replicate a proportional ratio, which the Greeks referred to as "The Golden Ratio." The shapes that are derived please the senses, possibly because of similarities to proportions found in the human body or other objects within nature. Pleasing proportions that have a universal appeal can be found in simple shapes such as the rectangle. They can be found in compositions of shapes placed together, the placement of pictures on walls, or even the combination of a group of pictures. Good proportion can be found in the sculptural feel of a three-dimensional object, and it can be found in a series of spaces, such as adjoining rooms in buildings or the combination of outside spaces created by buildings and landscaping.

Symbols and good proportion work together resonating deeply in the human psyche. Pinker explains, based on the developing theories of the new field of evolutionary aesthetics:

> As the visual system converts raw colors and forms to interpretable objects and scenes, the aesthetic coloring of its products gets even richer. Surveys of art, photography, and landscape design, together with experiments on people's visual tastes, have found recurring motifs in the sights that give people pleasure. Some of the motifs may belong to a search image for the optimal human habitat, a savanna: open grassland dotted with trees and bodies of water and inhabited by animals and flowering and fruiting plants. . . .
>
> Other patterns in a landscape may be pleasing because they are signals of safety, such as protected but panoramic views. Still others may be compelling because they are geographic features that make a terrain easy to explore and remember, such as landmarks, boundaries, and paths. . . .
>
> In good works of art, these aesthetic elements are layered so that the whole is more than the sum of its parts. A good landscape painting or photograph will simultaneously evoke an inviting environment and be composed of geometric shapes with pleasing balance and contrast.[13]

The beauty of architecture and its ability to evoke pleasant feelings depend on the quality of the composition of spaces, shapes, patterns, colors, proportions, contrasts and repetitions, and the way that together they resonate within each of us. We are born with natural preferences for proportion, and we develop some preferences by repeated exposures to images that take on symbolic meaning. Unsurprisingly, successful artists have had a talent for finding and using them, not dependent on scientific method but through sensitivity and a keen awareness of their own feelings and emotions. By the same token, all of us are born with an innate ability to express ourselves artistically using good proportion and symbolism; we just need the opportunity to develop our talent. And in a similar way, to fully enjoy music, painting, ceramics, sculpture or architecture we must simply be afforded enough opportunity within our daily lives to develop adequate sensitivity to feel their depth.

Sadly, the demands of a market-driven society based on mass production have marginalized artists and restrained our personal artistic expression. Our artistic side, our sensitivity to beauty and nature, and our emotional connection with architecture have been short-circuited by the unavoidable stream of stimulation created by technological gadgetry, communication devices, superfluous information, and exhaustive choices of entertainment. As a consequence, our avenue for creative and emotional expression and appreciation for our physical environment have faded. We sense the loss, but fail to recognize its source or for what we yearn. Instead, we try to quench our thirst the way we have been taught in our consumer oriented culture, with more and more mass-produced goods and entertainment which do not satisfy us but only serve to increase our disconnection and emptiness. These are doomed attempts to fill the void that used to be filled naturally by our personal artistic or creative expression and our continual exposure to the beauty of the world around us.

As we come to understand the dehumanizing deterioration of our artistic sensibilities, the full impacts of our assaults on nature, and the increased visual chaos, we must ask, "How do we recover what has been lost and set a new course for the future?" The beauty of towns and villages when people's lives were still compatible with the earth's life-support systems can serve as an inspirational beacon. The qualities of these places from the past can help us realize that we do not need fossil fuels to design an aesthetically rich and socially fulfilling world, and that we can live sustainably without sacrificing our quality of life.

Today when we get an opportunity to see the architecture Ruskin described before the age of fossil fuels, whether a cottage in a wooded clearing, a villa on a mountainside, or the silhouette of a village or town in the distance, we are often moved by its ageless beauty, feeling a delightful connection. Our pleasing experiences confirm a universal appeal that suggests we could be comfortable living in those places. The villages and towns that existed in Ruskin's day may, for many of us, be even more aesthetically pleasing and appealing than our own neighborhoods. This is not meant to suggest that life in earlier times was not more difficult, less humane, especially towards women and children, and filled with more inconveniences—and indeed peril—than life today, and there certainly were sights that were disturbing such as devastation left by war and natural disaster. But what people of Ruskin's day and before did have was a visual environment that consistently offered the beauty of visual harmony.

NINETEENTH-CENTURY PAINTING

Later, when we visit and contemplate the nineteenth-century towns and villages of Ruskin's day, we will get a glimpse of what the world looked like when human society existed within the limits of a healthy global ecosystem. We will see how, as Ruskin noted, integrity in design and visual harmony contributed to mental health, how identification with architecture created a sense of power, and how its beauty provided pleasure.[13] First, however, in order to consider our most basic relationship with nature and with architecture, and to understand what humans really need from both to live fulfilling lives, we must go back even further in history to a time when our ancestors were just beginning to expand the use of symbols and artistic expression in crafts, music, and architecture.

CHAPTER II

ARCHITECTURE
From a Bouquet of Dandelions to Plastic Flowers

PREHISTORY

Humans first arrived in Europe thirty-five to forty thousand years ago. They were people almost exactly like us. After leaving Africa sometime about fifty thousand years ago, they moved up through western Asia and then westward. Eventually, they entered into northern Europe, being referred to by anthropologists as Cro-Magnons. They continued to adapt physically and culturally as the climate of the Ice Age grew colder, reaching its peak around 20,000 BC.[1] They spent their time following animal herds, continually on the hunt for food. They foraged for roots, greens, nuts, seeds, leaves, and berries—anything that could sustain them. From these distant ancestors, who lived in crude shelters and fought the harsh elements during the Ice Age, as well as people to the south and east facing continuously changing environmental challenges, we inherit our emotions, our intellect, and our ambitious character. It is with these qualities and dispositions that we react to nature today and create and respond to the architectural environment we live in.

Architecture and planning in Europe had their beginnings as these early people moved from one location to another. Evidence from archaeological sites allows us glimpses of where and how these people lived through the centuries, but we can only speculate about what they were thinking and feeling and how those thoughts and emotions evolved and led to art and architecture as we experience them today. What kind of feelings and emotions linked those early humans to what they crafted and built?

When I picture myself living as my ancestors did in the earliest of those times, about 2,200 generations ago, I imagine myself trying to find campsites with strategic advantages for defense from predators, sites that provided protection from the elements or had other features that would make life more comfortable. I would be attracted to places that offered panoramic views or had distinctive visual features that appealed to me. I would look for sites that had access to water and to materials for building shelters. When I could, I would lodge in the mouth of a cave. Most of the time, however, I would live in temporary structures that my family and I made from some combination of branches, limbs, bark, reeds, stones, earth, and animal hides.

For thousands of years, each family built its own shelter. It was a repetitious task, but the challenge of figuring out how best to use the available materials made it enjoyable. We were accomplished at using our hands and imaginations in building and took pride in our work. We found special ways to build and decorate that appealed to us and distinguished us from others. I can see myself laying rocks around the perimeter of my newly built hut in the pattern I always use, and my little daughter handing her mother a bouquet of dande-lions to hang over the entrance. When our task was completed and night fell, my family would gather together in our shelter, feeling comfort and safety as well as a sense of accomplishment.

A fire would have been the focal point of our camp. It was an evening event that occurred in the wilderness almost every night for hundreds of generations. Eventually cooking became a ritual because we enjoyed some foods better when they were cooked and knew when something needed to be cooked to keep us from getting sick. The flames of the fire kept animals away, providing a sense of security. When it was cold, the warmth from the fire provided comfort and extended time for conversation, music, and working to-gether making and repairing tools, weapons, and clothes.

During our early European existence, humans lived in small groups most of the time, occasionally coming together in large groups when food sources were concentrated, such as herds of reindeer and spawning salmon.[2] When we came into contact with other groups roaming in the region, there was a feeling of excitement if we knew them and had a rapport with them. If we didn't, we were cautious, fearing hostility and committed to defending our territory.

Humans had developed an efficient means of cooperation for hunting, gathering food, building shelters, making clothes, and de-fending themselves. They spent most of their time next to meadows, streams, lakes, or seashores. In these places they performed the daily activities necessary to sustain themselves and provide comfort, and here is where much of our recently acquired genetic makeup evolved. It should be no surprise that today we still find time spent in natural environments calming and comfortable and that some of our deepest feelings and emotions come from the basic relationship we have with nature, our personal shelters, hearth, fire, and intimate family.

During the thousands of years when population densities were low in Europe, early humans would have tried to avoid physical conflict and killing unless they had no other choice. It was risky and took energy away from the everyday demands of surviving under the often harsh climate and ever-present natural dangers. With so few people, every potentially capable individual was valued because he or she was needed to increase the chance of survival of the group. Our cooperative nature, a necessity for success in our evolutionary path, continued to develop as our language skills improved.

On the occasion when people came together it was usually to trade, glean information about food sources, find marriage partners for our young adults, or satisfy our curiosity about others. When we got together we saw new ways to make and decorate clothes, tools, and shelters. Over time, our campsites became more elaborate. Language became more expressive, as did the art in our clothing, tools, weapons, rituals, and shelters. Brian M. Fagan states in *World PreHistory*:

> These adaptations developed rapidly, indeed spectacularly, after thirty-five thousand years ago. It was during these millennia that Homo-Sapiens finally mastered winter, for it was in northern latitudes that human ingenuity and endurance were tested to the fullest. The Cro-Magnons of western and central Europe developed elaborate and sophisticated hunting cultures during this period. Their cultures were marked not only by many technological innovations, but by a flowering of religious and social life, reflected in one of the earliest art traditions in the world.[3]

A rich diversity of cultures developed, becoming more varied and sophisticated as time went on. From an evolutionary standpoint, diversity in the way we lived also increased the chances that some of our groups would survive through the extreme cold spells, food shortages, and floods that periodically occurred.

For thousands of years humans were forced south from their most northern habitat by the advancing cold weather and ice. During this era our cousins the Neanderthals could not adapt or compete and ceased to exist. By 20,000 BC, humans had spread across much of the world, genetically similar but with varied cultures resulting from the unique conditions from region to region and continent to continent. In his book *After the Ice*, Steve Mithen describes early humans based on archaeological findings dating between 20,000 and 5,000 BC:

> All people in all continents at 20,000 BC were members of Homo sapiens, a single and recently evolved species of humankind. As such, they shared the same biological drives and the means to achieve them—a mix of co-operation and competition, sharing and selfishness, virtue and violence. All possessed a peculiar type of mind, one with an insatiable curiosity and new-found creativity. This mind—one quite different to that of any human ancestor—enabled people to colonise, to invent, to solve problems, and to create new religious beliefs and styles of art.[4]

The art that had been evolving for thousands of years included carved animals and intricate carved decorations and designs on bone and wood tools and weapons. The designs may have been derived from patterns in trees, flowers, animals, and rock formations, and used to identify the artists as individuals or as members of a clan, or for some other symbolic meaning. Early humans decorated the hides on their shelters with painted images, they carved figures in wood, and they placed wood, stones, and animal bones in unique patterns. At gatherings with other clans and groups, they would have seen the carvings on their tools and weapons, the jewelry they wore, and the paintings on their clothes and shelters. The art would have elicited respect for its creators and inspired viewers to find new ways to express themselves. Art may have been the most significant material expression of human identity, and this intrigue with decoration and ornamentation and the symbolic meaning it conveyed ultimately found its way into everything they built—their architecture.

Starting 30,000 years ago and reaching its peak about 15,000 years ago, humans were drawing and painting with beautiful proportion in line and color. They were recording on the walls of caves

PAINTED BISON - ALTAMIRA CAVE, SPAIN

images of the animals they were hunting, outlines of their hands, and special symbols. Shamans may have relied on these paintings to give them power and authority, or to impress others and to gain their allegiance. They may have used the paintings in rituals to help their clans build confidence for upcoming hunting excursions. The purpose is not clear, but the creativity and talent were exquisite. Mithen explains:

> The tradition of painting and carving animals, especially horse and bison, together with abstract signs and human figures, had lasted for more than 20,000 years. It had extended from the Urals to southern Spain, and produced masterpieces by the score: the painted bison of Altamira, and lions of

Chauvet, the horses of Lascaux, the carved ibex from Mas
d'Azil. For more than 800 generations, artists had inherited
the same concerns and the same techniques. It was by far
the longest-lived art tradition known to humankind, and yet
it virtually disappeared overnight with global warming.[5]

Around twelve hundred years ago as the glaciers in Europe began to retreat and the climate was warming, life became easier, and
the population started to expand. By 8,000 BC, the people to the
east in the valley of the Tigris and Euphrates rivers were cultivating
grains, allowing for more specialization of work and higher densities
of people,[6] but Europe was still predominately settled by hunter-
gatherers. Barry Cunliffe, in his book *Europe Between the Oceans 9000
BC-AD 1000*, writes:

> [They were] Mesolithic hunter-gatherers who expanded
> through Europe, moving further and further north as the last
> cold period ended around 9600 BC. By 7000 BC these ad-
> vanced foragers had established themselves in most parts of
> the continent, adapting their food-gathering regimes to the
> different ecological niches they chose to inhabit.
>   By about 4000 BC the mobile hunter-gatherers inhabit-
> ing the forests who had followed their food sources as the
> seasons determined and others living in the lusher and more
> varied environments of the major river valleys, the estuaries
> and around the coasts, foragers with a more sedentary life-
> style, had been transformed into more agrarian lifestyles.[7]
>   . . . . In all but the most northern and eastern reaches of
> Europe communities had become food producers, cultivating
> crops of grain and herding domesticated animals-activities
> that called for a far more sedentary mode of existence based
> on village settlements occupied over many generations. It
> was a dramatic transformation. Mesolithic hunter-gath-
> erers were replaced by Neolithic food producers and with
> the new regime came the "Neolithic package"-ground stone
> tools, pottery and rectangular timber buildings, together
> with domesticated sheep, goats, cattle and pigs, and culti-
> vated cereals.[8]

Independent invention in language and art was occurring within groups and then being spread from one group to another. The

spread was from both the influx and movement of people and the exchange of ideas between groups. Those who had the greatest ability to adapt and ability to move on when necessary had the greatest chance of survival. Cunliffe writes:

> The rapidity of the spread of the Neolithic way of life was remarkable. While there can be no doubt that the indigenous Mesolithic populations played an active role, contributing massively to the gene pool of the emerging farming societies and providing an ambiance of mobility, there was also an inbuilt ethic of pioneering that drove the early farmers inexorably forward to the limits of Europe, by land, through the deciduous forests of the north, and by sea, land-hopping through the Mediterranean to the Atlantic. We have suggested that this dynamic may have been embedded in a system of social values enshrining the belief that young men could gain status only by leading colonizing expeditions. This may well be, but perhaps behind it all lay an innate desire to explore the unknown, drawn on westwards by a curiosity to discover the wonder of the setting sun. All speculation, of course—but then we are dealing not just with settlement plans and pottery distributions but with real people with aspirations and hopes.[9]

As agriculture spread, permanent settlements became more abundant. Having a permanent village made it easier for a people to protect their lands and provided new incentives to invest more in their own shelters as well as in community structures. There was a more stable food supply due to the ability to store the harvest in protective buildings, and a sense of power and pride from the more elaborate permanent structures. The hamlets and villages offered safety to their inhabitants because of the larger number of people living there.

The move to the village seems to have prompted two important changes in the way people lived. According to Peter Wilson, in his book *The Domestication of the Human Species*, the first was that large numbers of people lived in close proximity, with personal property such as permanent houses with yards and shared structures set aside for community activity. This kind of community required that people's activities be organized and coordinated. The second change involved an increase in fighting over prime land, either to protect it or to seize more, and the development of defense and attack strategies. Increased population densities provoked tribal competition for land, game, and resources. The aggressive side of human nature became more of an advantage as the more powerful and intelligent drove off or assimilated the less capable. Cunliffe writes:

> By the Late Mesolithic period warfare had become a common reality. Perhaps aggression was exacerbated by increased competition for resources. As the hunter-gatherer communities grew, population in some areas may have reached the holding capacity of the land. In coastal regions, particularly around the North Sea and the Baltic, the problem would have been made more acute by a rapid rise in sea levels driving people from traditional foraging grounds. Another factor could have been social tensions resulting from communities deeper in the heart of Europe beginning to adopt a sedentary way of life associated with the Neolithic food-producing economy. Whatever the reasons, for the foraging societies of the Late Mesolithic world warfare was now an everyday reality.[10]

As land was secured and protected, the evolution of village life and the architecture of permanent structures began. Peter Wilson sees "the change from nomadic life to living in permanent villages and consequently the beginning of more permanent architecture as human domestication, the second major adaptation defining humanity after we left the forests to live on the plains."[11] Wilson indicates that at this point in our history humans began to control nature rather than live a lifestyle that constantly responded to it. Wilson believes that the move to the village was compelling because it "provided the facilities for enriched or heightened social life at the same time as it offered the means and instruments for keeping the social life under control."[12] Cunliffe, on the other hand, believes that in addition, eligible young women would have been more attracted to a mate in a permanent village because of its apparent stability. Architecture—the physical ingredient of the village—in most instances consisted mainly of houses, their accompanying yards, some pattern for the layout of the village, and, often out of necessity, protective walls.

STONEHENGE

As time passed, the village became more complex, with sites or structures for community rituals and specialized work. Artistic expression was found in everything that was being made or built, and human ingenuity was constantly creating new inventions. Cunliffe points out,

> In the structure of buildings and the arrangement of settlements there is a general sameness—houses were usually rectangular and timber—built and were grouped together in hamlets or villages—but different social systems led to variation and distinct regional vernaculars began to appear.[13]

Along with the move to the village, more sophisticated forms of artistic expression in clothing design, body ornamentation, music, and architecture continued to evolve. Houses, community buildings, and village layout often used culturally unique symbolic patterns reflecting spiritual beliefs. Individual identity was reflected in the decoration of houses. Village-wide characteristics reflected the spiritual and artistic values of the community.

Artistic expression was interwoven with spiritual beliefs, customs, and rituals for dealing with fear of the unknown, concepts of the afterlife, social organization, and beliefs about our connection to nature and our attempts to exert control over it. Structures were built and places selected specifically for ritual and spiritual activity. In very early times these were caves, altars, and burial sites, but as time passed, they expanded to include special shelters, stone dolmens, tombs, and ultimately temples, churches, mosques, and cathedrals.

From as early as 8,000 BC, some groups were making difficult, time-consuming efforts to build stone dolmens or earth mounds of different sizes and patterns, sometimes built together and sometimes separately. By 4,500 BC, more elaborate dolmens were being built, such as Stonehenge in southern England. These efforts did not meet the immediate needs of shelter, food, or clothing, yet the significant time and group effort involved in their building indicates that there was some kind of powerful incentive. Construction of a monumental project, whether early dolmens or later cathedrals, provided laborers the reward of knowing their efforts were integral to

CARCASSONNE

its creation and gave them pride of identity with its existence. They could work with enthusiasm when they could see the completed vision in their mind's eye, and know that it would leave a legacy for the future. Peter Wilson suggests:

> In return for their labor the people were provided with a spectacle, a sight, a creation that rivaled, if it did not outdo, natural landmarks. . . . Once established, the monument exerts an effect on those associated with it, as builders, officiates, congregation, or plain onlookers. In this way the power embodied in the monument is felt as a living force within the individual.[14]

As our ancestors saw the vision of the dolmens take actual form, they must have felt a sense of power and control over nature individually and as a group. Many of the stone monuments relate to the movement of the sun, moon, and stars, connecting the people to the earth's cycles. Success in the prediction of seasons and celestial events affirmed their society's knowledge.

With a growing population in Europe, fighting and war over land and resources continued to escalate. As the aggressive nature of humans became more prevalent, architecture had to take on the added function of protecting people from the dangers of attack. Hilltop forts were built for strategic defensive advantage, sometimes near farming communities and sometimes with an extensive system of walls incorporating the farms. Walled settlements became the norm, continuing beyond the Celtic period into Roman times and throughout the Middle Ages, as exemplified by Carcassonne in southern France. Architecture that was defensible provided inhabitants with a sense of safety that lowered the stress of fear. When seen today, the walls around medieval towns add to the beauty of the town but not without ominous overtones, adding a chill to our feelings as we are reminded of our violent nature and history.

By about 4,000 BC experimentation with metallurgy—primarily copper and gold—had begun. By 2,000 BC, copper and tin were combined to produce bronze, an invention that started a new age and charted a new course for human society. The use of these metals, while occurring throughout Europe, advanced fastest in the region around the Aegean Sea. The Minoan culture, centered in Crete, and the Mycenaean culture that developed later brought considerable advances in the use of the metals as well as advances in painting, ceramics, and architecture. Regional differences evolved as tech-

LION GATE

nologies of metallurgy spread throughout Europe, just as they did in methods of building. On the island of Crete, palaces surrounded by houses and other buildings added a new dimension to urban settle-ments. Between 2,000 and 1,000 BC more sophisticated palaces were built by the Mycenaeans. The Lion Gate on the Citadel Palace of

Tyrians, built around 1250 BC, remains as a reminder of the elegance of the artistic expression of that culture. In their book *The Bronze Age in Europe*, Jean-Pierre Mohen and Christiane Eluère elaborate:

> The Mycenaean world, consigned to oblivion until the excavation of its great sites brought to light its grandiose architecture and refined craftsmanship, symbolized the pinnacle of the Bronze Age in the mid-second millennium. Nevertheless, even the glory of Greece could not eclipse those other civilizations—every bit as remarkable—that left their mark elsewhere in Europe.[15]

The Bronze-Age culture fanned out from Mycenae across much of Europe. Trading posts were established and trading routes connected them, tying together the cultural areas of Europe. Mohen and Eluère lay out the factors behind the dynamism of Bronze-Age cultural areas in Europe: a) The exploitation of raw materials, such as Baltic and English amber; copper in Ireland, England, southern Iberia, the Alps, the Erzgebirge in central Europe, the Carpathians, the Caucasus, and Cyprus; and tin, in Cornwall and southern Brittany; b) Trade, by sea and river, in the Baltic and the North Sea, along the Atlantic, in the Mediterranean, in the Black Sea, and in the Danube Valley; c) Hierarchical social organization that favored artisanship, such as the palace system in Greece and Sicily, the fortified camp system throughout central and western Europe, and the system of large farms in the Nordic region.[16] As the technologies of metallurgy spread through Europe with the regional differences in design evolving, so it was with architecture.

THE CELTS

While the cultures around the eastern Mediterranean were generally more advanced, a culture to the north was solidifying across Europe with unique and beautiful artistic expression. In *The Celts*, T. G. E. Powell describes these people as "the first Great nation north of the Alps. . . fascinating forerunners of the historical nations of northern Europe."[17]

Their culture, or cultures associated with them by their art and building, once extended over nearly a quarter of Europe, from Aus-

tria across France to the British Isles and down into Spain and Por-
tugal. The earliest archaeological finds date Celtic culture back to
before 900 BC, when the Celts emerged from the Rhinelands of central Europe as a dis-
tinct group of tribes.[18]
The culture spread
through the varied
peoples across Europe.
By 600 BC proto-Celt-
ic cultures of the Hall-
statt period, so named
after archaeological
finds in a cemetery
in Hallstatt, Austria,
had spread through-
out most of France and
Spain. By 400 BC, a
new Celtic style had
emerged, known as
the La Tène culture,
named after archaeo-
logical discoveries
on Lake Neuchâtel in
Switzerland, possibly
influenced from as far
away as Britain and
Ireland, where its in-
fluence remained the
longest.

In *Celtic Ornamen-
tation: Art of the Scribe*,
Courtney Davis writes:
With its characteris-

GRAVE MARKER

tic abstract symbols, floral patterns, and imaginative decoration, the
distinctive La Tène style was to provide inspiration for the artists
who created the illuminated manuscripts and intricate stone carvings in Britain and Ireland over a thousand years later.[19]

Remnants of the culture still exist today and can be seen in the language, detail in art and architecture, and even grave stones in Ireland, Wales, Scotland, England, Brittany, and Gaelic Spain.

Archaeological evidence reveals that across Europe these highly varied tribes of warriors, farmers, and artists had a history of rival warfare among themselves as they competed with their Celtic neighbors for resources. Most were just skirmishes between warrior chiefs for honor and disputed land and did not inflict much damage on the general population. Protected by their warrior chiefs, who lived in centrally located hill forts and controlled grazing territories, the people farmed and raised cattle. Archaeological excavations show that houses were built by sinking wood poles into the ground with a roofing framework attached to the uprights. Woven branches were used for side walls and thatch for a roof covering. The houses were generally rectangular in France and central Europe but round in the British Isles and on the Iberian Peninsula, where some shelters were also made of stone. Powell describes their organization as a type of stronghold or town:

> A number of house foundations bespeak a large social and economic unit, sometimes possibly a chieftain's household. . . . More particularly, the special siting and greater size of one or two buildings may indicate the overlord's residence, and this is well exemplified in the Urnfield culture defended site at Altjoch on the Kochel Sea, in Bavaria, where a single large rectangular house occupied the inner fortification, below which stood the smaller houses and farm structures. Similarly at the Hallstatt culture site on the Goldberg, in Württemberg, a rectangular post-build house, and another large building, stood within a timber stockade, outside which were more than two dozen structures of varying kinds, both houses and other farm buildings, the whole having been included within an outer fortification.[20]

Powell goes on to point out that the Celts' settlements were growing in size and prominence:

> The sites so far mentioned were essentially rural, but considering large permanent settlements, such as the Languidocian oppida, we must suppose that the normal Celtic

social system had undergone some modification, and this must certainly have been true of the great "townships" of Central Gaul, such as Gerovia, Bibracte and Avaricum.[21]

By 400 BC, the Celts living in what today is France turned their excess energy and an oversupply of restless warriors to the outside, invading the Greeks, the Etruscans, the Macedonians, and the Romans. These actions were part of the beginning of a more serious and dangerous cycle of violent struggle among people throughout Europe and Asia, continually intensifying as populations grew larger. For most of the Celts, this cycle ended in their cultural demise.

THE GREEKS AND THE ROMANS

As we look back to see where architecture and city planning blossomed, we find that it happened in the same cultures where laws and knowledge grew and spread under what we now call Western civilization. How then did humanity move from stone huts, pole structures, and hill forts to villages, towns, and cities built well enough to last for centuries? The answer lies in the cultural adaptations of group organization and control, and the balance between self-interest and sharing.

In his book *The Republic*, Plato refers to a statement by Socrates:

> Until Philosophers rule as kings or those who are now called kings and leading men genuinely and adequately philosophize, that is, until political power and philosophy entirely coincide, while the many natures who at present pursue either one exclusively are forcibly prevented from doing so, cities will have no rest from evil. . . nor I think, will the human race.[22]

Socrates' statement reveals first of all that philosophy, in his mind, is based on truth or simply goodness and that evil will prevail in the absence of good kings or leaders. History has provided us with examples of both. His statement also refers to the city, which in other translations of *The Republic* is called the state (either one meaning the city-state). The city-state was the social organization that allowed for the development and maintenance of the great cities and their control of nearby farmlands and resources. The city-state was the social unit by which society was organized, and where democracy had its roots.

It was due to the organization and facilitation of effective government within these city-states that individual citizens had the time, education, and resources to reach a higher level of potential in science, philosophy, art, politics, construction, education, and medicine. The philosophical views embedded in this system of governance valued the freedom of individuals and their rights within their society, creating a leap forward for humanity. Cunliffe, in his book *Between the Oceans 9000 BC-AD1000*, describes the times:

> Each citizen-state had its own distinctive ethos, and pace of change varied from one to another. Before 500 BC the most spectacular development in the Greek world took place in the cities of the western Anatolian coast and north to Miletos in the south. Art and architecture flourished, developing new and highly original styles, and it was here that philosophy and science were born. Miletos in the sixth century was home to a succession of brilliant original thinkers, Thales, Anaximander and Aneximenes, men who thought about the world rationally and tried to understand it from first principles. The mathematician Pythagoras was a native of Samos, Heraclitus the philosopher came from Ephesus, Hecataeus, historian and geographer, was a Miletian, as was the townplanner Hippodamus, while the poet, or poets, we know as Homer may have come from Smyrna. The Dorian cities to the south were home to the fifth-century giants— Hippocrates, the physician who was born on the island of Cos, and Herodocus, fairly called the father of history, whose town of birth was Halicarnassus—It was a stunning cast, encompassing the greatest minds who created the basis of western civilization.[23]

The great accomplishments of this era were possible because government helped its citizens avoid ruin from the ever-present menaces of greed, maliciousness, and ignorance and created a fertile environment for thinking, arts, and architecture. Cunliffe explains:

> In Athens, for example, estimates based on cemetery evidence suggest that in 700 BC there were seven thousand

inhabitants, but within a hundred years the population had grown to twenty thousand. Towns like Athens and Corinth grew up in a haphazard fashion around their central sanctuaries. Gradually, however, through the seventh and sixth centuries BC, this was rationalized. In Athens the site of the agora—a large open communal space—was being cleared of old buildings in the mid-sixth century and defined by boundary stoned proclaiming 'I am the boundary of the agora'. Around the edges of the open space public buildings were now constructed including lawcourts, the council house, shrines and stoas (public walks). The creation of such a space, where the population could assemble and where the institutions of the state were now formalized in public buildings, can be seen as the final act in the long process that led to the fully functioning city-state.[24]

As European civilization entered the Greek and Roman ages of the city-states, a much more sophisticated and monumental religious, civic, and residential architecture developed, referred to now as classical architecture, in the form of temples, villas, shrines, forums, theaters, coliseums, and civic basilicas. But there was a fundamental difference between the Greek worldview and priorities and that of the Romans who followed them. Emil Ludwig, in his book written in 1942, *The Mediterranean*, wrote:

> The history of Athens proved that a nation may understand and cultivate wealth and the mind, commerce and beauty, at one and the same time. The pure will to power is one thing that makes any people barbarous in the long run. The fact that almost all the springs of our intellectual culture rose in Greece, very few in Rome—and indeed that the Romans as political conquerors of the Greeks merely became their pupils and heirs, taking over from them and coarsening literature, wisdom, and sculpture, without adding any brilliant innovations—proves the superiority of intellect to force, and allows us to draw hopeful conclusions in a time when barbarians are pushing forward anew.[25]

Sir Banister Fletcher, in his book *A History of Architecture*, explains the two underpining differences in the architecture of the two great cultures:

The Greeks, consciously or unconsciously, practiced extreme simplicity in art, and the fine-grained marble in which
much of their work was done encouraged the tendency to
leave purity of outline to speak for itself. Thus, whether on
the grand scale of a temple building like the Parthenon or in
the single human figure as the Hermes of Olympia, they were
content with beauty unadorned by distracting ornament.

The perfection of Greek art lies in its simplicity. The
Greeks were artists by nature, and Greek art was the outward expression of the national love of beauty.

The Romans never seem to have been satisfied until they
had loaded their monumental buildings with every possible
ornamental addition. Here too again the influence of material is apparent; for concrete demanded a disguise, and coarse
limestone did not permit of delicate purity of line and thus
called for extraneous ornament, so the Romans completed
the magnificence of their monuments by a wealth of decoration.

The characteristic of Roman art lies in its forcefulness.
The Romans were rulers by nature, and Roman art was the
outward expression of the national love of power.[26]

Ultimately, the growth of city-states and the interaction among
them led to territorial alliances, expanding empires, and competition among emerging philosophical, governmental, and religious
points of view. Powerful leaders would use the prevailing belief systems to gain a following and then justify their own desire to expand
their domain by denigrating those with different cultural, religious
or governmental systems, as Rome did when it emerged as the greatest superpower of its time.

Throughout history, the ethnocentric tendency in people—their
view of themselves as superior—has allowed leaders to foment na-
tionalistic fanaticism and hysterical thinking to support wars fought
for ideologies as well as for land and resources. The religious and
spiritual edifices of others then became the emotional targets for
destruction. After conquering a region, the victors would tear down
the temples or other places of worship, and the conquering people
would build their own temples or churches over the rubble of the
conquered. The Roman Empire did just that as it expanded across
the Middle Eastern, Etruscan, Greek, Macedonian, North African,

and Celtic societies. Ireland, parts of Wales, and Scotland were the only Celtic areas spared from the invading forces. As the Romans took over Celtic territories, the Celts gradually became assimilated. Their communal lands were divided for individual houses and agricultural uses, and substantial amounts of land were claimed by the government for civic functions.[27]

According to French historian P. Boisannade in his book *Life and Work in Medieval Europe,* as the Roman Empire expanded, based on the knowledge and technology acquired from the Etruscans, Greeks, and Phoenicians, new Roman towns were built with local governments that provided protection and justice through the power of the Roman State. As the Romans built towns, they cleared forests, drained swamps, and brought the land into agricultural cultivation. Roads were built to provide convenient travel, and great aqueducts brought water to where it was needed. At the height of the Roman Empire, ninety thousand miles of roads connected seventy-one provinces and hundreds of towns.[28] The Roman Empire brought a long period of relatively peaceful stability to its domain, where in some places protective walls were not necessary. A social life flourished in the towns and villages. Public squares, circuses, theaters, baths, marketplaces, and temples formed the basis of social activity, occurring in new architectural forms brought from the classical world of Rome, Greece, and Byzantium. In the Roman countryside, villages, houses, and villas were surrounded by cultivated agriculture, including grains, fruit trees, vines, and olives as well as livestock.

While there was an aristocratic class, there was also a middle class made up of merchants and artisans and a lower class of farmers, day laborers, and tenant farmers who nevertheless were also free under Roman law. By the end of the Roman Empire, slavery had almost entirely disappeared, replaced by more-productive free artisans.[29] As Christianity became the religion of the Empire, large parcels of land were set aside for the Church. It was not long before a new monumental architecture began to develop, producing variations in what is called the "Early Christian Style." The basilica was the model for new churches. Fletcher points out that "colour gave richness and glimmering mystery to interiors. The mosaics which lined the domed apses generally represented Christ, the Virgin, apostles or saints with all those symbolic emblems which now entered largely into decoration."[30]

By the time it fell in the fifth century, the Roman Empire had spread over nearly a quarter of Europe, including what is today the Balkans, Greece, Italy, Spain, France, Austria, Switzerland, parts of Romania, Hungary, the Czech Republic, Germany, and England. But three-quarters of Europe had remained tribal in nature, lacking the material wealth and power the Roman Empire had accumulated, and the contrasting Roman civilization was a target for their envy and aggression.

THE EARLY MIDDLE AGES AND THE GREAT MIGRATIONS

The Roman Empire had for nearly six centuries held back invaders, but between 406 and 416 AD it was mostly destroyed, collapsing from the attacks made by surrounding tribes and the internal decay of its own political system. Much of the Empire's progress was reversed as its territories fell under control of the invading anarchical tribes or became fiefdoms or small kingdoms. The ensuing three hundred years saw massive upheaval in the form of great invasions and migrations in which one group would push another out of their land. If they were not killed, the displaced either became the slaves of the conquerors, were assimilated, or took over new territory themselves. The artisans, laborers, and farmers generally ended up in servitude. Rome under the law established by the Caesars had gradually brought together all classes and all races in equality; with its demise, slavery reemerged. By the year 600, many towns had just a fraction of their former populations and were barely recognizable because of the destruction of their lands. Periodic famine appeared after droughts, floods, or the ravages of marauding bands.

During this time, the Huns moved from the East into Hungary and pressed westward. Slavic tribes were heading south into the Balkans. The Scandinavians were pushing south along the coast of Europe, and Germanic tribes were moving south into Italy and Spain and to the west toward Britain. Beginning in 711, the Moors in northern Africa moved north into Spain, bringing a new religion and cultural influences from the Mideast. They conquered much of

Spain, but in 732 were stopped at Tours, France, by Charles Martel, for the most part fixing the frontier between Christendom and Islam for the following three centuries.[31]

Having been referred to in the past as the Dark Ages this period certainly darkened the enlightenment of the Greeks and Romans and ushered in a period absent many of the previous achievements in hygiene, law, education, agriculture, and science. Throughout this period, the Roman Catholic Church maintained a small foothold in some areas, continuing to advocate for the weak, the peasants, children, and women, yet many people returned to pagan beliefs. It was only in the East in Byzantium that the Christian Church and government maintained major elements of Roman civilization. Some of the most significant developments in architecture during this period occurred in Byzantium. Though based on Roman architecture, Byzantine architecture distinguished itself by the use of domes to cover polygonal and square plans. The roof system of domes is quite different from the early Christian timber trusses and the later Romanesque system of stone vaults. The prevailing motif of the Byzantine is the dome, which came from eastern architecture and through the years would influence architecture throughout Europe.

The process of social and economic reconstruction was slow and sporadic and varied widely theough Europe. The land in each region ended up primarily in the control of small kingdoms or was left unclaimed. Within each kingdom, a new landed aristocracy developed, taking title to land and building the power and economic base needed to maintain its position. Eventually, many of the small domains that emerged out of the Early Middle Ages were taken over by larger and more powerful kingdoms, the power reverting once again to a distant authority. Some of those who did not become subjects of the conquering kings with their larger centralized domains survived in free fiefdoms or, in some cases, towns located in isolated areas throughout Europe.[32]

CHARLEMAGNE AND THE CAROLINGIAN EMPIRE

The defeat of the Moors at Tours, marked the beginning of the Carolingian Empire, ruled successively by Charles Martel, his son

"Pippin the Short," and then his grandson, Charlemagne. When Charlemagne took over rule from his father and grandfather in France, he solidified a central authority over most of France and then across much of what had once been the rest of Roman Europe. In 800 Pope Leo III crowned Charlemagne emperor. This public alliance between the pope and Charlemagne strengthened a growing political power in the west.

The coalition was the beginning of what would become the Holy Roman Empire, which dominated Central Europe throughout the Middle Ages and into the beginning of modern times. As a king and emperor, Charlemagne exercised supreme jurisdiction in judicial matters, made legislation, led the army, and protected both the Church and the poor. His administration was an attempt to organize the disparate kingdoms, the Church, and nobility around himself; his success was built on the efficiency, loyalty, and support of his subjects as well as fear because of his ruthless attacks during his conquest. Ultimately, Charlemagne's forces took over northern Italy, and under his rule the Huns were pushed back into Hungary. The Scandinavians were held to the coast of France, while some migrating German Saxons were deflected to the British Isles.

Between 600 AD and 900 AD the influence of the Church and of a scattering of dynamic rulers—particularly Charlemagne—brought about a gradual reinstatement of order and improvement in production and livelihood, including a more centralized economic system. Charlemagne unified the warring chieftains and reestablished roads and kept them safe. He restored markets and protected fairs and ports. Efficient and productive workshops reemerged in the villages, and rules protected and preserved the forests from wasteful cutting. In some places a system of relief for the poor was established.[33]

By the time of Charlemagne's reign, architecture's early Christian style was in transition. According to Fletcher in *The History of Architecture*:

> Basilicas or Roman Halls of justice probably served the
> early Christians as models for their churches, which form a
> connecting link between buildings of pagan Classic times
> and those of the Romanesque period which followed.[34]

The architecture of settlements was also changing based on new social structures. The systems that supported slavery and the brutal treatment of workers were being replaced with mini-kingdoms, where peasant workers and sometimes small landowners formed specialized economic units. According to Boissonnade:

> In the center was the master's villa or manor, kind of a half castle half farmhouse, incorporating stables, storehouses, cellars, workshops and chapels. The peasant, living in contrast to the extravagances of the lord of the villa, built his own house, with all family members participating in producing what was necessary for existence: food, furniture, and farm equipment by the men, baking bread and weaving flax and wool to be sewn into garments by the women. In the villas, the workers were specialized, laboring as millers, bakers, butchers, ironsmiths, goldsmiths, painters, and specialists in brewing, carpenters, ironworkers, weavers, spinners, rope makers, saddlers, soap makers and launderers. Great meals with entertainment for guests and hunting for sport became the entertainment of this class. With these efforts, they produced lavish lifestyles for their Masters with finely crafted architecture, furniture, clothing, and jewelry.[35]

During this roughly three-hundred-year period after the Early Middle Ages, wine-making became more prevalent than it had been since Roman times, with vineyards planted on the edges of villages. According to Boissonade:

> There was progress in restoring horticulture and floriculture, arboriculture and vine-growing, as monasteries, noble domains and farms increased cultivated lands and the variety of production on them. The vine, propagated by kings, nobles and monks, was reestablished in the eighth century on the banks of the Moselle, the Rhine, and the Danube. The wines of Spier, Worms, and Mainz had a wide clientele throughout these regions in the ninth century. In France the requirements of local consumption led to plantations as far afield as Neustria; Burgundy was already celebrated in the seventh century for its wines from the Côte d'Or, and Saintonge. The Bordeaux and Norbonne districts increased production of their sought-after vintages.[36]

The changes occurring in Europe were anything but uniform. From village to village, kingdom to kingdom, and region to region, some locations saw progress in the reconstruction of a civilized world while others nearby endured conquests by tyrants or the continued dominance of cruel and exploitative leaders.

In contrast, outside of what had been the Roman Empire, in lands where the Celts had lived—Scotland, Ireland, and Wales— life continued much as it had for centuries with the land in common ownership of the clans continuing their ancient customs. The simple communal society of those clans remained as they had been in earlier times which had been the norm everywhere.[37]

THE CHURCH'S HUMANITARIAN EXPANSION

By 900 AD, Christianity was expanding, gaining support not by its evangelism but for its humanitarian and economic enterprises. Hundreds of monasteries were created throughout Europe, with new agricultural communities emerging nearby. Free individuals and peasants alike seized the opportunities available in the growing communities. By the year 1000, the populations in many of the towns that had been part of the Roman Empire were recovering to their former numbers, and the new architectural expression of the Romanesque, with Roman and Byzantine influences, could be seen in the structures they built. New towns were also appearing near fortresses, fairs, and weekly markets. Fletcher describes how, from the remains of the Roman ruins—literally from the hewn stones, —buildings emerged, sometimes on the very foundation that had supported the grandeur of their predecessors. Architecture was evolving as the old fragments were transformed into a new art form and old methods were adapted to new needs. Fletcher wrote:

> The later Romanesque style of the tenth to the twelfth centuries was remarkable for the tentative use of a new constructive principle. This was the deliberate articulation of structure, in which each constructive part played a designed role in establishing equilibrium. This was in contrast to Roman construction, which had depended upon opposing uncoordinated masses. This new system, which was accompanied by the use of dressed stones of comparatively small size

COLLEGIATE CHURCH OF SANTILLANA DEL MAR

connected by thick beds of mortar, led in the thirteenth century, after many experiments, to the full development of the Gothic system of architecture, in which elasticity and equilibrium were jointly employed in the erection of the magnificent series of Gothic cathedrals. The general architectural character of the Romanesque style is sober and dignified, while picturesqueness depends on the grouping of towers and the projection of transepts and choir. It will be seen that in Italy, France, England, and Germany exceptional tendencies were brought about by local conditions; but in all these countries the character depends on the employment of vaulting, based on Roman methods.[38]

Feudalism, however, continued to be a force throughout Europe, and the aristocracy continued to seize much of the common and privately owned land for its own benefit. The feudal system was based on a hierarchy of landholders: kings, princes, counts, dukes, barons, knights, and squires. Within the feudal domains, certain soldiers and peasants would be given property for homes and agriculture in exchange for their services. At the bottom of society were the serfs, who made up well over half the population and whose lives were not much better than those of slaves.

The feudal system placed the common people, who toiled on but did not own the land, at the mercy of aristocrats. In some areas, though, town and village communities remained strong enough to withstand the pressures of the feudal powers and to help individuals maintain control of their properties.

The Church and its ideals moderated the effects of feudalism, with efforts to educate people, support individuals' rights against feudal lords, and serve as an example in their own communities.[39] According to Boissonnade, the Church spearheaded the expansion of schools for a broad range of people and founded higher education, which brought about a gradual improvement for the working man. By the 1200s, the Church—whose bishops retained control of their own domains, often guarded by their own soldiers—had accumulated a body of individuals whose talents helped create showplaces for more efficient agricultural methods and desirable environments for peasant life. The religious domains, with their vast land holdings, were developing agricultural science, including forestry, breeding, and the use of new crops and cultivation methods. The science of agriculture was reaching the levels it had attained during the Roman Empire. Rye, barley, oats, millet, and buckwheat were commonly planted. Wheat fields covered areas in Germany, France, Belgium, England, Spain and Italy, with rice also being grown in Mediterranean climates. Livestock almost always included sheep, pigs, and goats. Larger livestock were more prominent on estates; cattle provided milk and meat; horses were used for transportation and work and were bred for sale; oxen and mules pulled wagons and plows and were used to power grain mills. Common poultry included geese, chickens, guinea fowl, and peacocks, and bees were kept for honey and wax. Gardens grew shallots, artichokes, spinach, tarragon, and eggplant for market. Orchards in the warm climates provided oranges, apricots, figs, pomegranates, plums, lemons, almonds, and olives (mainly for their oil). In the north, apple and pear orchards were planted; vineyards thrived in every location and climate that would support them. During this time, French wines competed in renown with the best wines from Greece and Cyprus. Sugar cane was grown in Italy, Spain, and Provence, and hops in the Rhinelands and Bavaria. Oilseed plants were sources of lighting and food. Hemp and flax, and, in the far south, cotton provided industry with materials. Mulberries, used in silk production, were grown in southern Italy and eastern Spain.[40]

Towns that had Episcopal authority and monasteries taught the common people how to produce luxury fabrics, tapestry, embroidery, enamel and goldsmith's work, porcelain, glasswork, architecture, sculpture, and painting. The Church helped establish merchants around the centers of their domains and was instrumental in repairing and protecting roads, bridges, and infrastructure for water transport. The Church helped create markets and fairs, thus promoting and expanding the activities and aesthetics of medieval life.[41]

THE RISE OF TOWNS AND CITY-STATES

Although this era would not see the levels of civilization achieved by the Romans and Greeks, life became much easier for many people, and the building flourished with artistry in every aspect of design.

The prominence achieved by the towns and cities that managed to forge their own independence ensured that the beauty they created in their homes and civic buildings would last. It did and can still be seen today. Feudal society did not support local or regional commerce, because each domain produced almost everything necessary for life. As feudal landholders came under the jurisdiction of large monarchies, commerce expanded and the number of merchants grew. Centered in towns, these merchants were the basis of economic activity and power, much as they were during Roman times. This change solidified the urban form, optimizing it for economic activity. As daily and weekly markets expanded, the influx of new merchants, artisans, and professionals spurred the growth of commercial streets and the establishment of the market square. As international trade increased, merchants representing the various regions needed permanent locations for their warehouses and stores. Strategically located towns that were close to raw materials or on transportation routes began to grow into cities, clearly distinguishable from the smaller settlements. These new cities would eventually become the locations for manufacturing and industry.[42]

From 1000 to 1300 AD, interregional commerce and specialized industrial manufacturing—including linen cloth, rugs, drapes, saddles, weapons, armor, cutlery, and glass—developed, strengthening the reemerging towns, many of which had been Roman. In addition, the new levels of commerce and industry and an increasing population were generating the need for continued development of new towns; most of the towns and villages we see today in Europe have their roots in this period. The Gothic architectural style emerged during this time as well, with new building techniques and a more delicate and intricate form emphasizing carved stone tracery. Stone structures increasingly replaced wood-framed houses and were built with much of the same detail as monumental Gothic buildings.

Towns grew along roads or waterways as merchants built shops and houses next to castles or monasteries or at existing villas or hamlets. Across Europe many of the medieval streets remain. In some cases the streets appear to us today to have been laid out at random, but this is probably due to the contours of the site, to stands of trees that are no longer there, to springs or creeks or seasonal water swales that may or may not be visible, to market or fair sites that once existed, or simply to the arbitrary parceling of land to new owners. In some instances a more orderly form took shape based on predetermined grids that anticipated growth.

The growing number of merchants created a new vitality that attracted more and more people. Taverns and inns opened for business on the growing streets. Merchants became a well-to-do class,

NOTRE DAME

the bourgeoisie, many of whom had emerged from their status as peasants or artisans in servitude under the feudal system. The towns gradually became stable units, with all members leading comfortable lives. This slow process, occurring over 300 years in Europe, saw many struggles between the towns, which strove for autonomy, and the feudal lords, and in some cases even with the Church, which had enabled their very existence in the first place, but fought to retain control over them. The towns ultimately began to emerge as vigorous communities with their own systems of government and codes of inhabitants' rights.[43] According to Boissonade:

1380 GOTHIC RESIDENCE - CHIPPING CAMPDEN

They sought out new blood to enrich what they had achieved. They welcomed serfs, artisans and merchants who were given refuge and opportunity. 'Town air makes a man free' was a German proverb. The town offered freedom that had not existed before. One could marry; give his children in marriage at will; could move away; come and go; dispose of his property; acquire, possess, exchange, sell, will and bequeath his goods without permission of any authority.[44]

Some of the towns were granted charters under a national or state government, while others were free towns that owed allegiance to none; many of the latter were former city-states dating back to the Roman Empire. Each town strived to create a sphere of influence around it to secure land for the urban food supply, port frontage, transportation intersections, and other resources. In many cases, land was purchased or taken over for common use or to be leased back to peasants or for farms or estates. Boissonnade states:

> Thus beneath the gilding of romance which covers the history of the medieval communes, through the noise of the tumultuous life which was played out within their walls, in their public squares, under the shadow of their belfries and town halls, and amid all the fierce struggles of parties disputing with each other for power, there appears clearly a united, continuous, and realistic policy pursued by the urban states...its aim was to develop the power of production. The urban community, whether it was ruled by a bourgeois patriciate, by a democracy, or by bodies recruited from among the different classes in the city, was inspired by the same aims that had guided it in its efforts to gain emancipation. It pursued with untiring energy and rigid logic the maintenance and increase of its economic privileges, the enrichment of the community by means of organized work, so as to assure the power and greatness of the municipal state.[45]

Boissonnade paints a vivid picture of the aspirations and actions of the new town dweller:

> He imposed upon all, and especially upon the feudal class, if need be by force, a respect for the town peace, which was necessary for the safety of economic relations. He decreed the abolition of family wars within the city; he safeguarded the quiet of market, fair, and highway by rigorous rules. He succeeded in bringing about the triumph of the principles of equality, liberty, and order, so indispensable to mercantile and industrial societies. He placed them beneath the protection of the sacred symbol of the stone cross, which stood in every village, the visible sign of the new rights of the bourgeoisie.[46]

Increased access to education promoted greater success and more power for more people and shaped their attitudes toward a range of local issues. Leisure activities and architecture changed in response to the delight the newly educated class was taking in a growing range of intellectual amusements. Entertainers passing through towns and villages provided epics, romantic tales, plays, and comedies. Townspeople looked forward to processions, masquerades, fairs, and tournaments. Pageantry brought banners, food vendors, lively dress, and entertainers that immersed the town in music, color, and aromas. Squares served as venues for more than just the market, and theaters and halls provided space for the growing trend of indoor performance.

With the advent of the clock, economics became more efficient and life more punctual. In the 1300s, clocks began to appear on bell towers. Louis Mumford, in his book *Technics and Civilization*, points out, "The punctual ringing of the bells became the defining symbol of the urban town or village."[47]

Just like the urban environment, the surrounding rural countryside experienced great change, with new villages, sprouting up around larger towns. The surrounding peasants, landowners, woodcutters, and other skilled laborers provided the support for the vitality of the village. Peasants gradually acquired small properties and equal rights to the common lands and participated in the administration of the parish.[48] Boissonnade describes peasant life at the end of the 1200s:

> Never had the material existence of the peasants been so favourable, and to find such conditions again one must look onward to the middle of the nineteenth century. A multitude of new villages, townships, hamlets, homesteads, and farms sprang up, and a crowd of parishes. In France their number was unsurpassed for 500 years, and even diminished in certain parts during the centuries which followed. Here the peasants lived, sometimes in groups protected by hedges or walls of earth and rubble, furnished with watch-towers, sometimes scattered along the roads or in the midst of their fields, near their well or spring or pond and in the shelter of some valley or grove of trees. . . .
>
> The rural classes had also acquired a moral physiognomy in the new atmosphere of liberty and comfort, the characteristics of which gradually became more precise. The classes were not at all refined in their tastes, but the people were

cheerful and full of activity, loving the tavern, festivals, dancing, sometimes also dicing and other games of chance. They loved to listen to the tales and songs of minstrel or jongleur on the village green; on fair days they marveled at the juggler and the charlatan; and they lent a greedy ear to the sermon of the wandering friar or the gossip of the peddler, the living newspaper of that time.[49]

THE HUNDRED YEARS' WAR

The developing power of towns and the new freedom of their inhabitants grew as a result of infighting between the royal families in France. The Hundred Years' War was an intermittent conflict that lasted from 1337 to 1453 and took place between French and English forces in what is now France. The war was precipitated by the claims of some of the English kings to the French throne and ended with the expulsion of the English from France. These conflicts, gave impetus to the growth of both French and English nationalism.

The first conflict was known as the Edwardian War, which lasted from 1337 until 1360, when the Treaty of Bretagne was signed. This twenty-three-year period was marked by the victories of Edward III of England at the battles of Crecy and Poitiers. In the following years, English pressure brought France close to anarchy and civil war and finally forced the French signing of a humiliating peace treaty. It took only nine years for war to break out again. In May 1369 the Black Prince, son of Edward III of England, refused an illegal summons to Paris issued by the French king, who responded by declaring what became known as the Caroline War, which lasted another twenty years.

The Lancastrian War was the third war, commencing in 1415 when Henry V of England invaded Normandy. During that time England came to the height of its power in France, with Henry V being crowned the country's king. The war ended only when the English were finally driven from France by the forces of Joan of Arc.

During this dynastic rivalry, the role of the peasantry was changing from servant-worker to servant-soldier, creating the first standing armies in Western Europe since the time of the Roman Empire. French and English kings alike attempted to lure peasants to their side with concessions of power, thereby strengthening the peasant-ry's status in life. In some instances the concessions included the building of new towns, which provided the peasants with more free-dom and opportunity to improve their lives.[50]

THE RENAISSANCE AND THE REFORMATION

The effects of wars and of the Black Death—the menacing series of plagues that began in the mid-1300s and that took the lives of over half of Europe's population—drove the progress of civilization back-ward again until the late 1400s. At this time, as power was increas-ingly consolidated into centralized nations, people came to depend on a distant government to ensure their freedoms and administer civil law, and shifted their loyalties accordingly.[51]

Meanwhile, following a new intellectual movement spread by the writings of Dante, Petrarch, and Boccaccio, a renaissance in lit-erature and architecture began to spread northward from Italy. Me-dieval art was rejected, and the art and ideas of Leonardo da Vinci and Michelangelo gained influence. In architecture, Roman facades became popular. Banister Fletcher notes, "Buildings began to be treated very much as pictures, largely independent of an expression of structural necessity, which had been the controlling element in medieval times."[52] From the 1500s through the 1800s, Gothic archi-tecture increasingly gave way to a highly varied Renaissance archi-tecture and its Baroque offshoots, influenced by the vast cultural differences throughout Europe.

The Renaissance affected the power of the Church as well. In 1517 Martin Luther, an Augustinian monk, published his *Theses on the Power of Indulgences*. Luther and other Protestant reformers attacked the Roman Catholic Church's beliefs and practices, including pur-gatory, particular judgment, devotion to Mary, the intercession of the saints, most of the sacraments, and papal authority, touching off what became known as the Protestant Reformation. An evangelical humanist named Jean Cauvin (Latinized as Calvin) began a move-ment in Switzerland as well.

The new Protestant movement touched off religious wars, divid-ed communities, and ultimately changed the dynamics of life in the towns that now had two different Christian denominations, Roman Catholic and Protestant. Protestant values emphasized the sanctity between men and women in marriage and denounced the loose morals associated with sexual activity before or outside of marriage or for purposes other than procreation. In 1530 King Henry VIII of England took advantage of the new religion's leniency on marriage and broke with the Catholic Church to create a Protestant Church of England that would allow him to annul his marriage.

THE BEGINNING OF THE MODERN AGE

The loosening of the Church's hold coincided with the emergence of a new worldview that began, in many ways, to challenge the fundamentals of Christianity. In 1637, Rene Descartes' book, *Discourse on the Method of Rightly Conducting the Reason and Seeking Truth in the Sciences*, started circulating through Western Europe. It immediately set off a furor by opponents to this new, "modern" way of thinking about self, nature, the world, our celestial surroundings, and mathematics. Descartes' Method, as it is called, stimulated and challenged other thinkers, influencing the greatest minds of the era—John Locke, David Hume, George Berkeley, Isaac Newton, and Spinoza.

For his work, Descartes is known as "the father of modern science." His concept starts with his approach: "never to accept anything for true which I did not clearly know to be such."[53] This new idea of skepticism influenced many to start discovering things for themselves rather than relying solely on authority.[54] Descartes said:

> Good sense is mankind's most equitably divided endowment. . .The differences of opinion are not due to differences in intelligence, but merely to the fact that we use different approaches and consider different things. For it is not enough to have a good mind: one must use it well.[55]

Russell Short, in his book *Descartes' Bones: A Skeletal History of the Conflict Between Faith and Reason*, points out how quickly the world was beginning to transform itself as a result of "Descartes' Method":

> Nitrogen was discovered, electricity harnessed, the first appendectomy performed. . . . The Hawaiian Islands were

discovered. The fountain pen was invented, and the fire ex-
tinguisher, the piano, the tuning fork, and the flush toilet.
Clocks, microscopes, compasses, lamps, and carriages were
refined. In the English city of Birmingham alone, the small
group of men who called themselves the Lunar Society, epit-
omizing the passion for combining invention and industry,
discovered oxygen, created the steam engine, identified digi-
talis as a treatment for heart ailments, and built the world's
first factories. Men caught in the grip of a mania for collecting and classifying roamed the earth and gathered spiders,
minerals, fossils, and flowers. Museums, dictionaries, and
encyclopedias came into existence. Surnames—Watt, Fahr-
enheit, Schweppe, Celsius, Wedgwood—became products
or terminology.[56]

Church and government leaders alike feared the ramifications
of this new way of thinking, and for good reason: It spawned democratic revolutions in the United States in 1776 and France in 1789,
putting power into the hands of a broader part of civilization.

In architecture during this period, the Baroque style emerged
in Italy and spread to Spain, central Europe, and Belgium but made
only modest inroads into France, Holland, and England. It is interesting to note that this flamboyant style was less popular in the
places where the revolution in thinking brought about by Descartes'
ideas was strongest. Is there a connection between rational thinking and pretentious design? By 1750, when the Enlightenment was
well under way, architecture throughout Europe was turning back
again for inspiration to the Roman, Greek, and Gothic styles.

Entering the Industrial Revolution

For us to begin to see and feel what existed 150 years ago, when
Ruskin was writing *The Poetry of Architecture*, we must understand
the simplicity of life back then. Over half the population in Europe
still lived in small towns, villages, hamlets, single cottages or estates
in the countryside. Life for most, whether rural or urban, centered
around the home and the village or town. Most people spent their
days farming or processing food mainly for themselves or for the
town or village they lived in or near. For most, clothing was made

at home or by local seamstresses and tailors, and shoes were made by local shoemakers. Most material goods, from furniture to the materials used in building, were made locally or within the region.

Leisure time was spent in interactions with family and friends, discussions around the dinner table, games, and music, and individually in reading and meditative walks in nature. Most entertainment relied on personal creativity and human contact, characteristics that have been lost in the television and Internet culture of today.

People lived in close proximity to work and entertainment. Travel at that time was infrequent for all but the affluent. People walked, rode horses, or traveled in animal-drawn carriages or wagons to the market, work, church, places of commerce, and social events. Trains were just beginning to carry people and freight for distant travel.

When John Ruskin started traveling with his parents on the European continent in the 1830s, it was by mail coach. As he grew older and the family became more affluent, they hired their own coach, which allowed them to travel on their own schedule and to stop where they wanted. As Ruskin grew older and began traveling alone, he occasionally used the train but preferred other means, when available, to get to his destinations. He laments:

> In the olden days of travelling, now to return no more, in which distance could not be vanquished without toil, but in which that toil was rewarded, partly by the power of deliberate survey of the countries through which the journey lay, and partly by the happiness of the evening hours, when from the top of the last hill he has surmounted, the traveler beheld the quiet village where he was to rest, scattered among the meadows beside its valley stream; or, from the long hoped for turn in the dusty perspective of the causeway, saw, for the first time, the towers of some famed city, faint in the rays of sunset—hours of peaceful and thoughtful pleasure, for which the rush of the arrival in the railway station is perhaps not always, or to all men, an equivalent.[57]

During that era, industrial manufacturing of goods and architectural components, was just beginning to replace the work of local craftsmen and artisans, which was slow and laborious, but highly

valued. What was being lost was the value placed on artistic expression and craftsmanship, which had resulted in goods that not
only were of higher quality but were also produced with more diversity. This changing value would also begin to affect architecture.
These disappearing qualities had always given the user a deeper personal connection to architecture and the objects around them, and
had given the worker a sense of pride and satisfaction that cannot be
found in factories or on today's construction sites.

Since Ruskin's time, some villages and towns have seen only
modest growth, allowing them to maintain much of their pristine
character, while others, in an effort to provide housing and more
locations for new industries in the expanding economies, have experienced sprawling growth. People increasingly moved from the
pristine and picturesque villages and hamlets to the growing cities
in the hope of finding new opportunities. Many encountered inferior
working and living conditions, characterized by sparse, utilitarian
buildings, littered streets, and polluted air. A harsh and unsightly
environment of tenement apartments became the home of the lower
classes. At the same time, the affluent were being drawn to areas of
the city that were attractive and relatively clean—places that were
graced by grand parks and stately buildings and offered an abundance of entertaining social activities. In 1832 a cholera epidemic
swept through Europe, killing thousands, and was followed by periodic outbreaks of scarlet fever. With cities' rapid growth and higher
densities, the already crude sanitation systems quickly became even
more ineffective, making life for the lower classes more unpleasant
and disease more prevalent for all.[58] The smaller towns and villages
avoided many of the problems of the denser urban areas.

By the 1840s, Europe was changing more rapidly, and it would
soon feel both the positive and negative effects of corporate industrialization, urbanization, industrialized agriculture, and increased
centralization of political power. The steam engine and rail transportation ushered in the beginning of the transition from a civilization based on wood and water as primary energy sources to one built
on iron and coal and, ultimately, oil. The rise of the capitalist economy provided faster development, more food for those in the cities,
and a broader range of products. The continual changes challenged

society's ability to make healthy adjustments in family life and lo-cal social organization. Changes were occurring much faster in the larger urban areas than in the smaller towns and villages, where life continued similarly to the way it had for the previous five centuries. Town or village residents could still walk out their doors, take a deep breath of clean air, and in moments arrive in the town square for festivities, buy goods at the local shops, attend church services, or stroll through the countryside or along an adjacent stream or riv-er.

The growth of towns and cities—many with more that 100,000 people—left an increasingly smaller proportion of the population able to produce its own food. By 1868, only 80 percent of the food consumed was still home-produced.[59] Larger farming operations were founded or formed around large cities, where there was a ready market, eventually leading to large-scale holdings and the beginning of agribusiness. Small farm holdings or rent-paying peasant ten-ants of large landholders were still the norm in the countryside, but even this would begin to change as residents left to seek work in the cities. According to Christopher Harvie and H. C. G. Matthew, *in Nineteenth-Century Britain:*

> All this left rural society demoralized and neglected, with the passivity characteristic of communities in decay. Thomas Hardy's novels, whose span of publication (1872-96) covered almost exactly the years of the agricultural depres-sion, captured majestically the uncontrollable and distant forces which seemed to determine the fate of the country communities and their inhabitants .... The 'general drama of pain' which the Wessex novels depict was the disinte-gration of a civilization. Surveying his novels as a whole in 1895." Hardy observed, "The change at the root of this has been the recent supplanting of the class of stationary cot-tagers, who carried on the local traditions and humours, by a population of more or less migratory labourers, which has led to a break of continuity in local history, more fatal than any other thing to the preservation of legend, folk-lore, close intersocial relations, and eccentric individualities. For these the indispensable conditions of existence are attach-ment to the soil of one particular spot by generation after generation."[60]

Harvie and Matthew conclude:

> Nonetheless, the image of a happy rural past lingered in town-dwellers' minds: regardless of class, whenever they could, they lived in a house with a garden, and perhaps rented an allotment: they recreated the country in the town while ignoring the reality of its sufferings. Architecture and town-planning increasingly reflected nostalgia for the village, culminating in the Bournville experiment of Cadbury's, the Quaker employers, and in the 'Garden City' movement at the end of the century.[61]

The plight of the worker was changing, too. Throughout Europe there were uprisings of the working classes and attempted revolutions, a reaction to the exploitation by the new owners of industrial wealth and the indifference of unsympathetic politicians. Historian Gareth Stedman Jones, in his book *Outcast London: A Study in the Relationship Between Classes and the Victorian Society*, points to the difference between "sweated labor" born of industrialization and the "artisans" of old:

> The sweated labor was poor; the artisan usually was not. While the sweated man struggled for life itself, the artisan was responsible for most of the community's energy and inventiveness. He could become quite prosperous, too, as long as he remained healthy and the economy remained sound.[62]

With the poverty that resulted from the shifting labor demands of industrialization, reform movements and charitable organizations such as the Salvation Army, the Labour Party in England, and the trade unions organized, as they were encouraged by the work of Ruskin, William Morris, George Bernard Shaw, Robert Blatchford, and others. It was in this context that the Arts and Craft Movement began in Britain, later to expand across Europe and to the United States. In the book *Campden: A New History*, editor Allan Warmington writes of the movement, "Its ideals were a high standard of individual craftsmanship and utilitarian simplicity, in marked contrast to the heavily decorated factory-made articles which had become the conventional taste of the time."[63]

Ruskin believed that the craftsman should be able to express his creativity in every object he made, that mere imitation and replication were to be rejected. Both Ruskin and William Morris promoted the ideal of the medieval craftsman who lived at a time when there was no hierarchical division between the arts and the crafts and who had time to produce the finest work for even ordinary people. Some believe that what was destroying the world of the artisan was not the machine itself but rather the new industrialization that exploited and debased both producer and user.

A number of guilds were established to reinstate the artisan. Ruskin formed a utopian guild based on a form of romanticized feudalism. He backed the individual weaver, and this venture in the Lake District of England and its products became known as Ruskin Linens.[64]

As the century closed with a strong counterrevolution to industrialization by the arts-and-crafts guilds, Ebenezer Howard and others started the New Town movement, a counter to the appalling sprawl that was growing on the edges of European cities. Howard laid out his plan in his book *Garden Cities of Tomorrow*: "[The] plan for garden cities incorporated a unified system of community land ownership, greenbelts and a balance of land uses, including industry and housing for workers, industrial and residential balance, self government, and an intimate relationship between city and country."[65] Letchworth Garden City was one of these. On the drawing board before the close of the century and under construction in 1903, it succeeded in capturing many of the best qualities of the medieval town.

Unfortunately, those in charge of development during the twentieth century failed to grasp the value of Howard's ideas and transformed what had once been the art of designing and building into yet another assembly-line process that puts profit over quality of life. And so we inherit a world marked by a collapsing environment and the poor aesthetics of corporate-built housing whose ambiance is best symbolized by the plastic flowers that are so often used to accessorize its interiors.

However, as Howard and Ruskin did before us, we can again look to the past and be inspired by it. As we travel through Europe in the following chapter, visiting towns and villages, we will see a portrait of architecture whose artistic expression is highly evolved, places were residents are surrounded by beauty both inspiring and nurturing. The history of each place will show how dramatically things have changed through time, and how ideas and events shaped each town and village and influenced their unique designs. We will look at and try to understand the mystery of the symbolism in their architecture. As we proceed, however, let us bear in mind that we are doing this not for the sake of nostalgia, but because viewing our past allows us to envision the arc of history, an arc that will take us into a future that will change drastically again, challenging us, as people have been challenged in the past, to either adapt or perish.

PARTIAL MAP OF EUROPE
2006

(The route of the journey from Dinan to Southamton is indicated by the dotted line.)

CHAPTER III

THE JOURNEY
To See and Feel the Poetry

In the summer of 2006, I traveled for three days by train across the United States and then after a day in New York six more by ship across the Atlantic to Europe to explore the architecture of preindustrial towns and villages. This would afford me the long-awaited opportunity to see, imagine, and record as best I could what these places would have been like before the rise of industrial society and the cultural diversity of architecture began to disappear. I wanted to know how the people in these places survived, flourished, and endured from prehistoric times to the present and how the architecture they chose to surround themselves with reflected who they were and how they lived. For the following two and a half months I traveled to eighteen towns and villages, hoping to temporarily leave behind today's world where cultural differences are being transposed into a standardized megaculture , and to see and feel Ruskin's world of the mid-1800s. What follows is my account of that experience.

I chose the towns and villages I visited because they represented a diversity of cultures and because most of their pre-industrial character had been preserved. In addition to the research I did before I left, I gathered information at each stop from local information bureaus and museums.

The photographs interspersed throughout the text have to the best of my ability, traces of modern times removed—including autos, signs, and people dressed in modern-day attire — through the use of computer magic; as a result, many of the photos certainly present a cleaner and more manicured appearance than the scene a traveler of 150 years ago would have encountered. As I visited museums throughout my journey, I studied paintings and early photographs of that era to confirm that my photos provided a reasonable depiction of the architecture at the time. I regret that there are no people in these photographs, for to truly see all the beauty of architecture and feel its emotional impact, one must see it alive with people carrying on their daily activities.

DINAN

Brittany - Dinan

I disembark from the ship at Southampton, England, and drive to Dover, where I take a ferry to Calais, France. It takes another day to get to my first destination. As I get closer to the town of Dinan after traveling through the dark forest of northwest Brittany—mostly hardwood trees and a lush, moist undercover—I notice on the rise to my left a stone farmhouse with red climbing roses branching up between the leaded glass windows. There is a vegetable garden and apple orchard above it and a field of grain sloping down to my right. I realize that a good number of farms are probably hidden from view by hills and forest, all working to supply vegetables, milk, cheese, and meat for themselves and those living behind Dinan's walls. Even though the sun is getting low in the sky, as I get closer to Dinan the forest seems more open and not as dark; it is apparent that trees are still being cut for firewood. This would have been the practice here for hundreds of years, yet the forests are still productive and healthy. Some of the local self-reliance that was a necessity in the past still seems to be present here.

With the sun setting behind me, I get my first glimpse of Dinan through the trees. The town lies just across a ravine where the Rance River widens into a small, narrow harbor. Stone houses with dark slate roofs lining the edge of the harbor are set back fifteen to twenty feet. In earlier times, the fleet of boats would have been returning at this time of day, after fishing or transporting goods back from the coastal towns downriver. I leave my car at the edge of town and walk across a small bridge leading to a cobbled street lined with half-timbered houses that wind their way up the hill.

Even though it is late afternoon, some of the doors are still open along the way, and I can hear people working inside. At one house the shutters are not yet closed over the front windows, and crafts are on display on the granite ledge.

The street's cobblestones are laid right up to the front walls of the houses, so plants are limited to window pots and the occasional

clump of grass, flowers, or vines growing out of cracks next to the houses. Where courtyards are shielded by walls along the street, I see moss, delicate flowers, tiny ferns, and succulents growing from between the stones, watered by the frequent Brittany rains.

As I make my way up the street and through one of the town gates, I can hear someone practicing a violin through the open window of an upstairs bedroom. The vaguely familiar

STONE WALL

melody becomes lost as I hear the sound of hoofs clattering on the street somewhere behind me. Five small boys pass me, shouting and running through an opening next to the edge of the ramparts and up to the wood plank walkway above. As evening fires are lit and the sweet aroma of wood smoke begins to drift through the street, something that feels familiar resonates deep inside me. I see the glow of a fire through a front door and hear it crackling. I imagine for a minute what the warming comfort of the fire would be like when coming in from one of the dark, cold, foggy nights typical of Brittany's winters.

During the cold months, the fires burn most of the day, heating the houses and the stonework surrounding the fireplaces. After the fires

TOWN GATE

have died out, heat from the stonework continues to radiate into the rooms late into the night.

EARLY MORNING ROOFTOPS

I reach my accommodations, which are in a family home halfway up the hill. Early the next morning, as I am looking out my third-level room toward the harbor below, I hear family members speaking in a language that is not French. Over breakfast, I ask about the language, and am told by my host that on occasion some people in Brittany still speak Breton, a Celtic dialect very close to Welsh and Cornish.

The language arrived here during the fifth and sixth centuries, when Celtic people migrated into the area, driven out of the British Isles by Anglo-Saxon invaders. The Celts intermingled with the native peoples, who were probably related to the early continental pagan Celts. The newly arrived Catholic Celts, who brought their religion from Roman Britain, became dominant, giving the kingdom its current name—Brittany. Brittany maintained its autonomy over the years but only through the fortune of military success and some timely royal marriages. In the late 1400s Brittany was still independent, with its own king and proud traditions, but in 1532, a treaty was signed, making Brittany a permanent part of France since that time. There have been struggles to maintain the language and traditions that grew out of the merging of the native pagans and Catholic Celts hundreds of years ago.

Around Dinan, there are many stone circles which are thought to have been used for early Celtic rituals. While Celtic peoples may indeed have adopted these circles for their own use, archaeological evidence has confirmed that they date back three to four thousand years earlier. When the Roman empire advanced northward, it built a road around the peninsula of Brittany, which was then called Armorica but that there is no evidence of significant Roman influence on the native people, who appeared to have kept their autonomy until the arrival of the Catholic Celts. At that time, Dinan was just a small settlement on the edge of the Rance River.

In the late 1100s the Roman Catholic Church took an interest in this part of Brittany and started the first of many building projects, providing the financial investment to make Dinan a thriving town. Did the Church choose this site simply to secure a domain in this wilderness area? Or was it to reform the Celtic Catholics, who, through intermingling with the local pagans and their traditions, may have been slipping ever further from mainstream Roman Catholicism?

The Church's investment in the area exemplifies its power and its effect in shaping the economy and architecture of towns and villages throughout Europe in the Middle Ages. Sometime in the 1100s, building began with the Saint-Sauveur Basilica, the first large church built here with money from the pope. With the new population of laborers, monks, and friars and a growing need for more merchants, a protective wall was built to provide safety and legitimacy to what was becoming an important town.

After breakfast I begin to walk through the town, noticing the abundance of greenery, an indication that the early inhabitants valued setting aside space for trees and plants. The largest area is a garden to the north overlooking the Rance. Other small squares and the large market square are connected by a grid of streets that run north to south and east to west.

Merchant and government buildings face the Place du Guesclin, named after a local knight, where weekly markets have been held through the ages. I am fortunate to be here on market day, to feel the charged atmosphere created by the large crowd of people and experience the sights and smells of the produce, meats, fish, baked goods, and clothing. For a moment I feel caught in a time warp as I realize this festive event has been occurring regularly for centuries.

In the center of town, there is a mix of houses and merchant and church buildings. Most of them date back to the 1200s and 1300s. The earlier houses were built with stone walls and fireplaces on each end extending to the roofline. The front and back walls were built with stone rising only to the second level. The floors above on these two sides are supported with wood-timber framework. In these half-timbered houses, the second level usually hangs over the first floor into the street by several feet. Molded and carved wood embellishes the overhangs and the doors and windows and is sometimes used as a transition between stone and timbered walls. The efficiency of their design can be seen in how quarried rectangular stone was used to provide strength at the corners and a straight edge around window and door openings for mounting the wood frame, and less expensive rubble rock for filler between the quarried stone and the timbers. Even though the houses are the same in their basic form, every house has its own unique characteristics, down to the patterns in the leaded glass. The ground floor in most houses appears to be used for work but also for cooking, eating, and entertaining. Access to the second level, where the bedrooms are, is by a steep, very narrow spiral staircase. All the houses have yard space to the rear or a side court for storage and animals.

SAINT-SAUVEUR BASILICA

After a fire spread through the thatched roofs of the town in the late 1700s, causing considerable damage, a law was passed requiring all houses to have slate roofs. As a result, the brown-gray thatch that had covered roofs here ever since prehistoric times gave way to slate tiles of multiple hues of black, gray, blue, and brown.

HALF-TIMBERED HOUSE

The more recent buildings reflect Renaissance and Baroque styles. The new and old architectures, a mix of the half-timbered houses and the newer all-stone houses with plastered surfaces, complement each other with pleasant variations and repetitions in materials. In the center of town most of the buildings have four levels, with the windows on the top floor in dormers placed on the steeply pitched roofs facing the street.

As I leave Dinan early in the morning after a two-night stay, I am curious to know where the design concepts and technologies originated and how they were passed down through the generations.

RENAISSANCE STYLE HOUSE

I am also curious about the absence of discernible Celtic symbols in the architecture. Perhaps they don't exist, or maybe I simply was unable to recognize them. My impression is that the older architectural style, from earlier Gothic times, possesses an honesty of expression in its materials and detailing that I find somewhat lacking in the later Renaissance style. While still quite attractive, the later style relied on a bit of pretence, as its plastered protrusions on the corners imitated the hidden quarried stone underneath. Regardless of its style, the durability of what has been built in the preceding centuries and the master builders' consistency in producing works of wonderfully pleasing proportion leaves the beholder with a sense of permanence stability and aesthetic delight. When I am well out

CHATEAU NEAR BRITTANY BORDER

of town and viewing a handsome chateau with a small hamlet at its edge, I am struck by the image (a symbol) of wealth and power of people who live independently of the hardships and struggle of the townspeople and likely without some of the joys of the commune.

Bastides: Domme and Montpazier

From Dinan I head southeast toward the town of Sarlat. Late in the afternoon, as I stop for food, I discover in my notes a friend's suggestion that I had overlooked. I change course and head toward Domme and Monpazier, two towns built in the late 1200s and born of unique circumstances. They were two of the more than three hundred new towns that were either begun or built in this region of France in the 1200s and 1300s to accommodate a tremendous surge in the population of Europe. Existing cities and towns were becoming overcrowded, due to the influx of a large roaming population that had been joined by people trying to escape repressive servitude. A succession of French kings was in a heated competition with their rival, King Edward the First of England, whose fiefdom lay within France, over the control of territory and resources. Both kingdoms were trying to consolidate the feudal holdings of their respective dukes, seigneurs, counts, and clergy, most of whom were imposing their own political will on the people in their domains. By building new towns in strategic locations, the rival kings were able to create new sources of revenue from taxes and new outposts of political and military power that could help fight the advancement of rival armies. The population of serfs, freemen, and hopeful merchants—who would otherwise be landless—came for the opportunity to own land as town walls were being built. The walls provided security from outside aggression and protection of the order within.

These new towns, called *bastides*, which originally and literally meant "market shed" but ultimately came to mean a fortified town, were built mostly in previously uninhabited areas of wilderness, which left many of them isolated and difficult to reach. The French and English kings both ordered the bastides to be laid out in a uniform fashion, with a central square and a grid system of streets based on ancient Greek planning concepts. The bastides were provided with charters, by-laws, and regulations for a government hierarchy and taxation, all of which created a certain commonality among them. The growth of these towns was part of the phenomenon that would lead to the creation of the bourgeoisie, the French middle class.

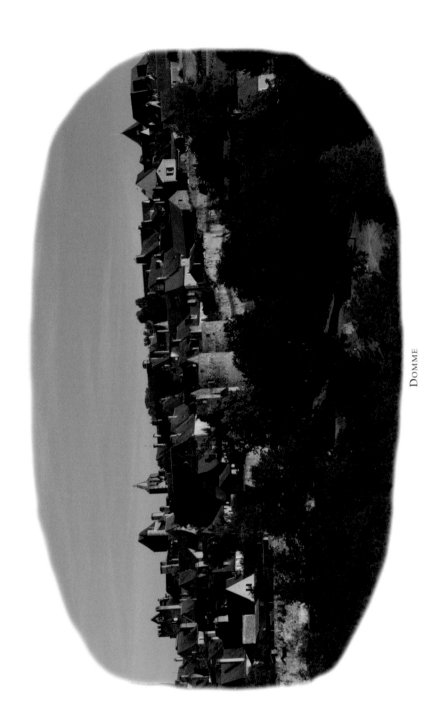

DOMME

Domme

Making my way along the Dordogne River, with a high sandstone cliff on my left, I note a difference in the kinds of trees and forest understory that indicate a drier climate than I'd found in Brittany. I wonder how the architecture will reflect the change in climate. As I round a corner, the clear, still water of the Dordogne provides perfect reflections of the sculptured sandstone cliff rising above it. The overhanging trees along the opposite shore also cast reflections of their arching limbs, and behind them are fields of grain with an occasional line of poplar trees. Finally, I get a glimpse of Domme in the distance, high up on a promontory on the far side of the valley.

I cross a bridge, then pass several farmhouses and finally climb up a road that traverses a side slope next to the perch on which Domme rests. As I approach the gate, the protective wall to my left ends at a sheer drop-off. To my right, outside the wall where a small ravine separates the town from an adjacent ridge, rock terraces provide spaces for gardens and fruit trees.

As I enter the town, which has a population of about a thousand, the atmosphere is quiet and peaceful. People are working in their houses, on the terraced slopes, or down on the valley floor. As I begin my walk I imagine that 150 years ago, at this time late in the day, carts and wagons would have been clattering up the streets, through the gates, and into the courtyards of the farmers' homes. The farmhouses are built around courtyards, with small barns and storage buildings forming an enclosure. They are intermingled with

To the Valley Floor

the houses of merchants and tradesmen. Most are two or three stories high, with the upper level providing views out of dormer windows. As in Dinan, the living and working areas are on the first level and the sleeping areas above.

On one house, the well-crafted detail on the carved stone window casements of a pair of corner windows catches my eye, an example of the time and artistry builders once put into their labors. Not

STONE CARVED WINDOW CASEMENTS

DORMER WINDOWS

only is this kind of workmanship of aesthetic benefit, but the lasting quality pays economic dividends over the years.

As I look at the buildings, I see no differences that might be attributed to the drier climate here, yet there are subtle differences in detail. The steep roofs here are covered with reddish-brown clay tiles. In some instances flat stones cover a portion of either the top or bottom of the roof, seemingly left over from a time when the roofs were made entirely from the heavier stones. The houses appear to be quite old, dating from the 1300s' and are of stone construction.

The grid of streets and narrow foot passages through the bastide are rigidly laid out over the top of the hill, with the exception of a triangular section at the south end. The main square is located at the highest point. Government, commercial and residential buildings, including the governor's house and the town hall, stand at its edges, with a market building in the center. A small, unassuming church, Notre

Dame de l'Assomption, stands just outside the square at the north-east corner.

This configuration, with the church in a less dominant location just off the market square, is characteristic of bastides, symbolizing the towns' secular nature, placing commerce in the more prominent position around the square. The kings may have imposed this requirement in an attempt to reduce the Church's influence. Next to the church on its north side, a thick canopy of chestnut trees covers a small plaza, commanding distant views of farms and the meandering Dordogne River in the valley below.

MARKET BUILDING

Leaving the shade of the trees, I walk to the edge of the steep drop-off, which is protected by a stone parapet, and follow a path along its edge. The view draws me into an involuntary trance—an instant meditation that separates this place from the world beyond. A feeling of solitude comes from the elevation, the quiet, and the surrounding peacefulness of the distant scenery. There is something very appealing here—I wonder if it is a universal appeal among people—being on a height that commands a panoramic view. As I continue to the path's end at the lower edge of the walled town but still within its perimeter, I find gardens and an orchard of figs, apricots, cherries, pears, and apples.

It turns out that the wall around Domme was extraordinarily difficult to build. Its construction was set into motion when the French King, Phillippe II le Hardi, ordered its creation. He had purchased the land from the monks of Sarlat, a nearby town, in 1280 for Domme, one of the many bastides he founded. They had held the property since 1214, when the ville chateau of Domme was leveled by the forces of Simon de Montfort during the Crusades to rid the region of Catharism, an offshoot of Catholicism that the Church considered dangerous. The king wanted this site, with its strategic view, as a fortification to help hold his territories. The very qualities that made it attractive for that purpose also made it difficult to build the wall, which took thirty years to complete. The first inhabitants were poor and often discouraged, but the ability to own a home and a piece of land for farming was enough of an incentive to keep them working.

Apparently, even with its remote location, the town continued to be involved in religious struggles. In the 1500s the Protestants managed to climb the front precipice and burn down the Catholic church. Earlier, from 1307 to 1318, some of the Knights Templar, whose entire order was captured by King Philippe le Bel, were held in Domme until their execution. On the walls of their prison in the circular tower at the gate of Tours, they inscribed their unique symbols—distinctive crosses, crucifixes, the Holy Grail, and others—that can be seen to this day.

Wanting to split my allotted time between two bastides, I move on after only one night's stay.

MONPAZIER

Less than fifty miles to the southwest, where the precipitous heights of Domme give way to a series of low rolling hills, I make my way across what for many years was a frontier border between France and England.

In January 1284 the bastide of Monpazier was founded for King Edward the First of England by Jean de Grailly, who situated his bastide to command the road from the south of France into the region of Périgord. The land was obtained from Pierre Gontaut Biron of Chateau Biron, on the agreement that he would get a share of the

MAIN STREET

king's taxes. At that time, nothing was here but forest and the artifacts of Stone Age people, who centuries before had lived on this gentle hill, known as Mont Pajerii, probably attracted by the spring that bubbles up just outside the town walls. When I reach Monpazier I park outside the walls and walk from one of the two main gates to the center. The town's grid has been laid out on a fairly flat south slope with twenty-four-foot-by-sixty-foot parcels for shops and houses along the streets.

MARKET SHED

That pattern changes as I come to the market square, which is surrounded by buildings and has arched arcades on all four sides, typical of bastide planning. In the past the square would have been kept well shaded and cool in the summer with a spreading canopy of chestnut trees. On the south of the square is a market structure built in the 1500s that is framed with chestnut wood and roofed with reddish-brown tiles. Under one corner of the roof a stone platform remains, holding three metal containers of different sizes. The containers were for measuring chestnuts or walnuts, which in the Middle Ages were used to pay taxes.

MARKET SQUARE

Just to the northeast of the market square and adjacent to a
smaller square is the church, Gothic in form and named after Saint
Dominique. Its reduced prominence is illustrated by its siting off
the main square, as is characteristic of all bastides, whether French
or English. I walk from the plaza down several streets. Most of the
windows on the houses are shuttered to keep the interiors cool. I
reach the most southeasterly building, once a large residence, but
now a museum with a large terrace garden that faces out across a

ST. DOMINIQUE'S CHURCH

parapet that is the top of a twenty-foot stone wall below to the countryside beyond.

MERCHANT HOUSE

As I look from the garden into the far distance, I can see numerous small farms that have been built over the past two hundred years. Nearer the walls are small rectangular farming plots separated by hedgerows. As their intricacy draws my attention, I see how they symbolize security by the food they provide. The family plots were parceled out to the people who originally made Monpazier their home, along with one of the personal dwelling sites within the walls.

There are subtle differences in the architecture in Monpazier from what I observed to the north. Here the buildings are made of yellow sandstone that weathers over time and takes on a grayish cast, gaining its richest character from green and brown mosses and patches of yellow lichen. Many of the roofs have a lower pitch, some with orange-red clay tiles and others with slates of reds, browns, and an occasional blue mixed together. Most of the roofs are hipped, and the chimneys are smaller. Extended beams or reinforcing tiles that offer additional support under the eaves are more prominent here, making some kind of a symbolic statement. As I look at the detail on the buildings I can once again see the individuality expressed by the local craftsmen. On a merchant's house at an intersection, I see a unique corner indentation left for the placement of a flowerpot or sculpture, and once again the carved stone on the dormer windows has its own design.

As I leave Monpazier, I think back to the sanctity and serenity I felt in Domme—a sense that my own spirit was lifted with the high vantage point—a feeling noticeably absent here, even though there are pleasant views out to the countryside. I wonder whether the feelings created by being elevated above one's surroundings is part of the reason we see so many early settlements built upon hills, ridge tops, or mountainsides. Or were these sites chosen solely for defensive purposes?

SARE

SARE

I drive south for a day to the Basque region and the village of Sare, with a population of about two thousand. It lies at the base of the Pyrenees on the French side of the border, near a point where the shoreline of the Bay of Biscay turns west and continues across the north of Spain. The land of the Basque people, found on both sides of the French-Spanish border, in ancient times extended beyond its current boundaries, united by those speaking the Basque language. Some believe the Basque are the direct descendents of the Stone Age people who lived here at least fourteen thousand years ago when tribal shamans were painting symbols and artistic representations of animals on the walls and ceilings of caves in the area. Linguists have found that the Basque language is unrelated to any other existing language and has only slight similarities to the most primitive Indo-European languages, suggesting that from Paleolithic times it developed independently of other languages.

Through the centuries, most of the Basque country was impenetrable. The people living here held off the Celts, traces of whose culture remain to the west, and the Romans, who penetrated only as far as the lands next to the coastline. As a result, the interior of the Basque region changed slowly and only by the people's choice, never through force of occupation. Christianity reached the coastal edge of the Basque region around 700 AD and only after centuries was accepted throughout the interior villages.

As I approach Sare, I stop and walk out into a field where I can get a good view of the village. Looking across the draw at Sare, I realize that this is the fourth town I have visited, and I now see that each with its unique design, its sculptural qualities, shapes and colors, and its gracefulness stands as an iconic symbol for its inhabitants. Its view for them must evoke a personal emotional connection involving pride, identity, and belonging—a sense of community and home. The image I see as a visitor, the beauty of each place, helps me gain a better sense of the people who live within.

The visual image of settlements, beginning with their earliest forms, would have been similarly evocative for their inhabitants, symbolizing the protection and security they offered and the pleasurable community rituals experienced within. This communal setting is where for centuries people prepared food, sewed clothing, made tools, and cooperated to defend themselves against predators and outsiders. These activities would have forged a bond between people and the places where they lived, a bond that is probably more significant than most of us realize. What of our potential and personal growth do we lose today if we are unable to connect emotionally to an appealing visual image of a town or village in which we live, a connection that is enlivened and enriches us each time we feel its symbolism?

VILLAGE CENTER

I enter the village now with these thoughts, feeling the spirit of the people as I watch them go about their activities. In the center there is an elongated plaza surrounded by houses, a store, and a tavern. At the far end is a court for playing pelota, a popular Basque sport descended from a handball game that began in the Middle Ages. The court is flanked on the left side by a vista to the countryside and

ST. MARTIN CHURCH

on the right by a terraced seating area for spectators. The surface of the plaza was historically covered with compacted decomposed rock. This plaza is also used for dancing and festivities, all integral to Basque culture.

Through a narrow street opening on the southwest side of the plaza stands a church that was built in the mid-1600s. Its exterior reflects the appearance of the houses built during the same period, a time when the marriage of King Louis XIV of France to Maria-Theresa of Spain brought considerable economic energy to the region. As with most Basque churches, the interior includes dark wood-framed seating balconies rising nearly to the ceiling on each side. The exterior of the church is whitewashed plaster over stone masonry. Large stones of irregular sizes on the buildings' corners and around the doors and windows are left in their natural golden brown color, creating bold abstract patterns. Most of the buildings now standing are relatively new compared with those in the other places I have visited, having been here for only several hundred years.

CHURCH WINDOWS

The houses in the village center are made completely of stone and have more refined workmanship than the farmhouses. The living areas in most village homes are on the street level. Farmhouses, on the other hand, are designed for storage and animals at ground level, and the living area is on the second level, with a kitchen and eating area next to a parlor and three or more bedrooms. In the past, being separated from the animals below by nothing more than a heavy plank floor provided warmth from the animals in cold weather, but at the price of having barnyard scent drift up through the cracks between the planks. A large attic is used for storing supplies and other belongings. At ground level is a recessed porch and

FARMHOUSE

just inside it is a large entrance hall with a wide double staircase leading all the way to the attic, making it easy to move harvested food and other items from ground level to the attic for storage.

Most farmhouses are half-timbered but differ from those I have seen to the north. These have low-pitched roofs with rounded clay tiles in variegated shades of red-orange, and no dormer windows. The houses usually face east to protect the entrance and balcony of the kitchen and parlor from the ocean storms that come from the southwest. The half-timbered walls rest on corbels (cantilevered beams) at each level, creating overhangs. The carefully quarried and chiseled stones used on the corners and for door and window frames have been left exposed, and the rubble rocks or wood and mortar between the heavy framing members are plastered and white-washed. The few houses have not recently been whitewashed or cleaned have a rich, weathered character.

STONE AND PLASTER

Some farmhouses in the countryside have been continuously occupied since the 1100s. They are primitive, without much of an artful display. They have one entrance for both animals and people and a few very small window holes. In early times, before glass became common, the holes allowed light in and vented the smoke from open cooking fires to the outside. Most have been remodeled with windows enlarged for glass and other improvements, including a fireplace, to make them more comfortable. But they remain less functional and comfortable as those built in the last three hundred years.

WEATHERED PLASTER

The buildings I have seen so far on my journey have shared the basic half-timbered and stone building technology, but there is diversity in room arrangements, fireplace and chimney designs, color, materials, and the multitude of ways the doors, windows, floors, and ceilings are

TWELFTH~CENTURY FARMHOUSE

detailed. The differences have evolved from some combination of the way people live, available materials, local invention, local culture, and the individual craftsmen's own creativity. I increasingly suspect that the basic building technology comes from a single source. Possibly the genesis was Roman house construction that spread through Europe during the expansion of the Roman Empire.

SANTILLANA DEL MAR

THE ALTAMIRA CAVE AND
SANTILLANA DEL MAR

Traveling from Sare to my next planned destination, Arcos de la Frontera in Andalusia, will require several days. Even though I'm concerned about my schedule, I find myself intrigued by the notion that the Basque date back to Paleolithic times, and I cannot resist taking a slight detour to visit the Altamira Cave near Santillana del Mar, where the drawings of animals and symbols on the walls and ceilings date back to prehistoric times. To protect the cave paintings, regulations have strictly limited access to a few visitors each day. Even though I will be unable to enter the Altamira cave, I will visit a replica built next to it, as well as the impressive Castalo Cave to the north. This should give me a glimpse of prehistoric life, hopefully shedding more light on how architecture was born as people learned to survive under constantly changing conditions.

I head west toward Santillana del Mar. It is a bit inland from the ocean in Cantabria. Further west lies Galicia, the Celtic state of Spain. The town of about a thousand people is near what was once a Roman road traversing northern Spain. In addition to its proximity to the Altamira cave, a substantial spring that provides a constant source of water explains why the site has been home to people for thousands of years, including monks who in the eighth or ninth century started a monastery here.

The opportunity for land ownership, granted in the 1100s by King Alfonso the First, as well as the Church's presence, helped Santillana establish itself as a regional center. The town continued to grow, with houses for merchants and residents and small palaces for the nobility.

From my hotel in town I set out for the cave, less than an hour's walk. My curiosity and excitement grow stronger with every step through the countryside, which is a vibrant green from the rains coming off the Bay of Biscayne. Had I been one of the prehistoric visitors to the cave, I would have seen from the cave's mouth a wide space that for thousands of years provided a commanding view of the surrounding valley, hills, and mountains. But no more. Around thirteen thousand years ago, shortly after the cave was abandoned, the overhanging ledge collapsed, blocking the entrance.

Though I cannot go inside, I stand before the cave, imagining what it was like when it was first discovered in the 1850s. Entering through a small excavation, I would have come into a dark room consisting of a flat floor with rocks laid together forming low walls to define different areas. It would have been lit only by candlelight and torches, and I would have felt awe, as I do now, in the presence of something dating so far back into the prehistoric past, a home for people still living during the Ice Age, working and moving around within the shadowy space. The cave's attendant and guard would have led me deeper into the cavern, where a multitude of different animal likenesses—bison, horses, and reindeer—were delicately, painted on the walls and ceiling with rich, subtle hues. I would have seen the outlines of hands and of what might be a human face, figures that possibly represent humans, and other symbols with no discernible meaning. Animated by the flickering light of the torches, the animals on the walls and ceiling would seem to move as I slowly passed by them.

I would have wondered about their meaning and the artists themselves. Were the symbols here painted by hunters with the magical objective of attracting game. Maybe they were intended to bring success and safety to the kill? Or were they the result of shaman artists painting in a spiritual trance to show appreciation for the animals that were killed for food? Were some of the symbols meant to bring good health or cure the sick? Whatever its intended purpose, the artwork is emotionally powerful and would have connected the people to the shaman or to deeply held spiritual beliefs. No doubt these paintings represent part of the evolution of art as well as spiritual expression.

But what about architecture? Is what I see here part of its evolution? From the cave's original large open mouth, extending a good sixty feet into its depths, the various-sized spaces created by the low stone walls were demarcations for different activities, possibly for use by different family units. Remains on the floor show that some areas were for making tools, others for cracking nuts or making clothes from hides, yet others for sleeping or group gatherings, with activities centered around one or more fires. As I consider the walls, which included a protective parapet at the opening of the cave, I decide that the cave is indeed part of early architecture, as its inhabitants designed the space to meet their specific needs.

ALTAMIRA CAVE

Archaeological evidence has revealed that fourteen thousand years ago these people had fairly well-tailored animal-skin clothing and musical instruments, such as whistles and pipes. The people who lived in the Altamira cave over a period that stretched more than four thousand years were blessed with far more protection and comfort than those living in smaller caves or makeshift shelters.

As I walk back to Santillana, impressed by what I have just seen and reflecting on the experience, I realize how special the Altamira cave was even at that time, and how envious visitors whose shelters were less comfortable might have been.

I arrive back in town and return to the task at hand. Here again, the architecture has its distinctive flavor. Golden-colored buildings made from quarried stone stand beside buildings that are plastered and white-washed, similar in color to those in the Basque regions but with more emphasis on elaborate wood detailing under the eaves. Coats of arms carved from stone are placed over the doors on the houses of nobility, a symbolic expression that has not been present in the previous towns I have visited. Three centuries ago, it

EAVE DETAIL

would have indicated the family's significant stature, perhaps attracting admiration from some and disdain or jealousy from others. Although symbolically they still imply status, today they mostly just add interest to the building and, when well composed and integrated, are visually pleasing.

The town's main street terminates at a plaza immediately in front of the Collegiate Church of Saint Juliana. Secondary streets lie on each side, creating an elongated grid pattern. One has a second plaza surrounded by houses of nobility, including the mayor's house. From the time the town was granted a charter in the 1100s, this plaza has been the location of a weekly market.

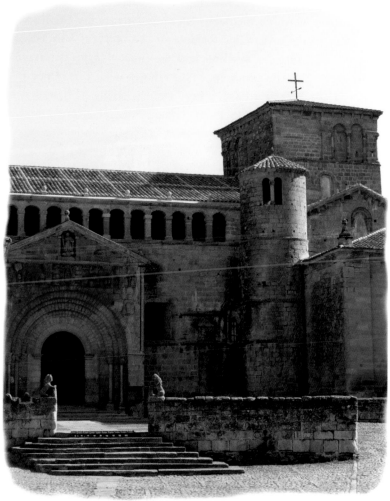

COLLEGIATE CHURCH DE SAINT JULIANA

Besides the attractive collection of grand houses and small palaces from different time periods, the most interesting architecture is the Collegiate Church, which was originally built in Romanesque style during the 1000s and 1100s, with a few additions since. The church feels different from any of the others I have visited. The inside is much darker, with the center aisle very narrow and the side columns proportionally larger, creating a more dominating presence. As I walk in, the small window openings above the altar do not let in enough natural light to allow me to clearly see the artwork or make out all the intricacies of the stone work. Over time, and with my movement through the dark aisles and side rooms, the flickering light from banks of candles on several tables eventually reveals a multitude of saints and symbols and the church's true character.

In some ways the experience is similar to what I imagined in the depths of the Altamira cave, where the flickering of flames would have created movement in every image—animal after animal and now, here in the church, saint after saint. The awe produced from the sublime experience and the complexity of the symbols in both places must have reassured beholders through the ages of the validity and power of their spiritual beliefs.

I am seeing with increasing clarity now how people have been emotionally connected to religious and

COLLEGIATE CHURCH DE SAINT JULIANA INTERIOR

spiritual spaces and buildings throughout history. The architecture of spiritual sites creates an emotional response, like the home and the village, and becomes part of a people's identity. But with religion, the ritual activities, which are meant to help people face their fear of the unknown or of death, to heal, to bring good fortune, to protect from enemies, or to help acquire special strengths, insights, or powers, have evolved in association with architecture. Through the centuries we have seen this expressed in dolmens, altars, shrines, temples, mosques, and churches, as well as from the multitude of iconic symbols incorporated into that architecture.

Despite knowing that religious symbols can generate fear and anxiety, exert a subjugating control, and even stifle reason, I cannot help but believe that the architecture of these places has played an important role in raising people's spirits and keeping them optimistic about the future. It is difficult to deny that through their beliefs or enlightenment individuals can be freed from worry and can approach life with a positive attitude—a frame of mind that benefits both physical and mental health.

CLOISTER

ARCOS

ARCOS DE LA FONTERA

Heading south over the Cantabria Mountains, a barrier that separates the northern coast of Spain from the majority of its land to the south, I enter a region that was controlled by the Moors for hundreds of years after they invaded in 711. Andalusia, my next destination, was part of a rich and fascinating civilization that emerged in Spain after the North Africans defeated kingdoms and bishoprics controlled by the Christians and Visigoths, who had invaded several centuries earlier as the Roman Empire crumbled. This area, I know by reputation, will look different from everything I have seen up to this point. The Muslims brought an architectural expression that was intricate, sensitive, and colorful in its detail and interior decoration, and they built an agricultural infrastructure that was more advanced than any other in Europe at the time. They grew rice, oranges, and a variety of other citrus fruits imported from the Middle East. Cordoba became the capital of the Muslim empire, with a population reaching five hundred thousand. By the 900s it had become the most prosperous city in Western Europe. Its territories included much of North Africa and the Iberian Peninsula, nearly a third of the whole Muslim world.

After a few days' drive, approaching Arcos de la Frontera in the valley of the Guadalete River, less than a hundred miles from Gibraltar, I look out over the hills and low mountains, which appear rugged, dry, and hot, with low-growing brush and few trees. Stretches of road are desolate—no farms, no herds, no people, just an occasional eagle or vulture. As I reach a mountain pass, Arcos appears before me in the distance on an outcropping, a high-rising island in the center of a patchwork of green and amber crops along the winding Gua-

dalete. The town, with its white buildings, looks from this distance like a large bank of snow, similar to distant views of many of the other white towns and villages on hills or the sides of moun-tains in Andalusia.

STEEP PASSAGEWAY

Once in town I make my way up the narrow pas-sageways that ran-domly traverse the slope. Some are so narrow that a don-key cart could bare-ly squeeze through, and at one point the street actually passes through the flying buttresses of one of the churches. I pass the main square at the highest point, where markets, festivities, and even an occasional bullfight oc-curred in the past. My hotel is nearby, just off the main square at the very edge of a cliff that plummets three or four hundred feet to the river below.

Late in the evening, after a meal and several glasses of wine, I read a verse written by a resident sometime in the past: "This rock that I live on sticking up out of the valley, making the river go around, has resisted the course of the river with the same stubbornness of the people who have lived here for centuries." As the town's name seems to indicate, Arcos de la Frontera was on the frontier of battles between the Muslims and Christians for centuries, but the history of the people here starts much earlier.

Small shallow caves carved into the limestone, the homes of Stone Age people, have been found in many places on the slopes of the hill. Archaeologists have also found small rock circles, the remains of the houses of people that lived here two hundred to a thousand years BC. Based on artifacts found, these people very well could have been a part of, or at least influenced by, early Celtic culture.

STREET

The invading Romans built their town, Arx-Arcie— meaning "fortress on high"—over the remnants of the round stone huts. They occupied the hill for an estimated two to three hundred years before the collapse of the Empire. Like the rest of the Roman Empire, the town was left without protection or organization, vulnerable to plundering and invasions. The migrating Visigoths from central Europe ultimately took control.

The Muslim invasion of the Iberian Peninsula spread from the south in 711. The ensuing five hundred years of wars and temporary alliances between the Christians and the Muslims and even between

ST. PETER'S PARISH CHURCH

warring Muslim kingdoms made this region famous, with tales of
knights, castles, and chivalry.

Under Moorish rule Arx-Arcie became Medina Arkosch, and the
town grew and prospered as the Moors built their houses and fortresses on top of Roman ruins, just as the Romans had built over the
Celts' houses hundreds of years before. For three hundred years Arcos remained the most important center in the area, weathering the

changing Moorish leadership and alliances and fighting off rebels and even Norman pirates from Scandinavia.

In the 1000s and 1100s, Arcos became the Kingdom of Taifas, first under the rule of its own Muslim king and later of Seville. By the mid-1200s the Spanish were purging Andalusia of the Moors, and the Muslim caliphate government was overthrown by King Alfonso of Castile.

The people here have had more than their share of conflicts, as late as the mid-1800s, roaming bandaleros and a general air of inhospitality beyond the town walls, in addition to the areas infamous harsh winds kept people on edge. Even the congregations of the two grand catholic churches argued over which church was the most important in Arcos. The only escape from the aggravations seem to have been in the refuge and serenity of the private inner patios of each home.

Influenced heavily by the architecture of the Moorish dwellings, Spanish builders designed houses around a central court that is open to the sky. The entrance is off the narrow street where there is a vestibule, with a second door opening onto the court or patio. The kitchen, bathroom, and living rooms are on the first level, with windows facing the street or the patio. A staircase rises up the side of the patio to balconies that provide access to the rooms above. Often there is a flat roof on the second or third level, creating additional patios with parapets around them. People keep goats and a few chickens on them. Cisterns have been dug into the ground-level patios, and pipes from the roof gutters drain into them, providing a water supply from rain. Almost every house and building has been painted white, except those that were built completely from quarried stone. The white walls reflect the sun's rays, cooling the interiors and patios significantly.

In the 1800s the phylloxera fungus wiped out the local vineyards, devastating the town economically with the loss of its main crop. In an effort to make ends meet, people took in those who could no longer afford their own homes, sometimes resulting in as many as four or five families living under one roof.

The exteriors of most of the houses are stark, with only a few windows and an entrance door, but entries and patios have colorful

PATIO ENTRY

displays of tile on the floors and wainscoting. The patios, usually adorned with many potted plants, are shaded most of the day, allowing the space to remain cool, a comforting retreat from winds

PATIO

and the hot Andalusian summers. In the more elaborate houses I find
the doorways framed by decorative carved stone with coats of arms
above; similar displays of carved stone can be found built into the

SOLARIUMS

patios. Some houses have been remodeled with glass-enclosed balconies, apparently a more recent architectural innovation that spread through Spain during the 1800s. The design offers a way to capture sunlight, a solarium providing auxiliary heating of the spaces inside during sunny days in colder weather as well as an additional buffer from nighttime temperatures. In the summertime, with the windows closed to the house and the solarium windows open, the glass-enclosed balconies function as a barrier from heat. I'm not sure of the date of this innovation, but it was a valuable concept for energy-efficient building.

Despite early Spanish attempts to destroy the Muslim buildings and symbols, the street layout and courtyard design that was originally brought from Arabia and North Africa remains. Ruins of houses from some of the oldest human settlements on record, found in Egypt and Mesopotamia, show this same pattern of an internal courtyard, differing only in that the houses were built with mud bricks.

The farms out on the flat land around Arcos have also been built around a rectangular patio that is enclosed by the house, storage and animal sheds, and walls. With their vineyards and pastures, livestock, citrus and grains, date palms and field crops, the farms still supply food to those who live on the Arcos rock.

THE ALHAMBRA

GRANADA AND THE ALHAMBRA

The road to Granada winds through more of the rugged hills and mountains of Andalusia, desolate in some parts but cultivated in others with farms and groves of olive trees. Occasionally on a distant hill I see the ruins of a Moorish castle. Just before reaching the historic town of Granada, I pass through a sprawling urban area on land that, according to historians, consisted of vineyards, vegetable gardens, and fields of grain as late as the 1800s.

In those days, when approaching Granada, it was possible to see the Alhambra rising on a hill above the town at the base of the snow-capped Sierra Nevada on the river Darro. In 1832 the American writer Washington Irving visited Granada, writing about all he saw and felt. His book, *Tales of the Alhambra*, gave the world a romantic description of the legends, traditions, and beauties of the palace-fortress and its accompanying city. Irving's stories inspired me, along with many other visitors from afar, to travel to Granada and witness firsthand the sites that inspired his enchanting descriptions of the people, history, and architecture. A favorite passage came to my mind as I approached my destination:

> From the lower end we passed through a Moorish archway into the renowned Court of Lions. There is no part of the edifice that gives us a more complete idea of its original beauty and magnificence than this, for none has suffered

COURT OF LIONS

so little from the ravages of time. In the centre stands the fountain famous in song and story. The alabaster basins still shed their diamond drops, and the twelve lions which support them cast forth their crystal streams as in the days of Boabdil. The court is laid out in flower-beds and surrounded by light Arabian arcades of open filigree-work, supported by slender pillars of white marble. The architecture, like that of all the other parts of the palace, is characterized by elegance rather than grandeur, bespeaking a delicate and graceful taste and a disposition to indolent enjoyment. When one looks upon the fairy tracery of the peristyles and the apparently fragile fretwork of the walls, it is difficult to believe that so much has survived the wear and tear of centuries, the shocks of earthquakes, the violence of war and the quiet, though no less baneful, pilferings of the tasteful traveler, it is almost sufficient to excuse the popular tradition that the whole is protected by a magic charm.[1]

COURT WITH POND AND WATER CHANNEL

Once I find lodging, I make my way to the Alhambra. As I wander about I can see that Moorish architecture, at its purest here, clearly wears an expression of its own. The vision of water and gardens, colorful tiles and filigree, the delicate arch work along passages, doorways, and windows, as well as filtered light from intricately carved screens, is sensuously hypnotic. I can see how these Moorish details have inspired the work of architects through time, who with appreciation for their beauty incorporated them into their own work. I discover one beautiful setting after another. Rooms are softly bathed in filtered light. Courtyards appear through arched windows. A

PATIO DE LA ACEQUIA

long rectangular pool offers ever-changing reflections of the plants, buildings, and sky. The sights and sounds of moving water, the deli-cacy of color, the proportion of the spaces, and above all the play of

FILIGREE ARCHES AND PATIO DE LA REJA

light and shadow created by delicate screens or by small openings in
the walls or ceilings of the rooms create sensations that range from
stimulating and intriguing to mesmerizing and relaxing.

ALBAICÍN

After getting a view across the Darro River from a portal, I head to the Albaicín neighborhood for another look at the Alhambra from a distance. I climb the streets of the Albaicín, which dates back to Moorish times, to a small plaza next to the Church of San Nicolás, and from there I quietly gaze at the bold yet graceful buildings set below the snow-capped Sierra Nevada mountains.

Prehistoric people lived on the hill where the Alhambra now rests. Before 1000 BC, the indigenous Tartessian tribe had a village here on the slope above the Darro River. Archaeologists have found that houses with walled yards were once scattered around a central fort of logs and rock walls, with an attached corral for animals. The houses were very small, round or oval in shape, and made of stone with one opening for an entrance. Central posts supported a ridge

ALHAMBRA

beam, while stick thatch covered the rafters. In the center was a fire pit, and around the sides a built-up seat or work counter. Evidence was found of kilns, which would have been used for baking pottery. The Alhambra stands in vivid contrast to the Bronze Age village that came before it. I wonder whether the Moorish kings felt more contented surrounded by the grandeur of their palace than the people who lived there six thousand years earlier did in the midst of their stone homes. Certainly their houses, stockade, and other buildings would have pleased their artistic sense, and they could not have conceived of anything like the Alhambra as a comparison to diminish personal satisfaction with their own efforts. Such thoughts lead me to wonder about our modern times: So many of us live in homes of extravagant size and comfort, yet to what extent do they add to our quality of life? Maybe the greatest pleasure and happiness comes from using our artistic talents in building, furnishing, and maintaining our shelters, with size and grandeur only providing marginal benefits. Certainly for the visitor there is a difference. The Alhambra sets itself apart from most other architecture by its sheer extravagance.

I leave my meditation and walk back down the narrow streets of the Albaicín to the local museum to learn more about the history here. The early inhabitants were ultimately subsumed by the Celtic culture. By the 500s BC, the Greeks had established a colony here and subdued the Tartessians. Although the Romans later took over the Iberian Peninsula, the whole of what is Spain today, establishing the authority of Roman Cordoba, they did not play an important role in this particular area's development. Between 62 and 64 AD, Christian apostles settled here. Ethnic and cultural influences by the Visigoths, Byzantines, and Jewish settlements continued after the fall of the Roman Empire. After the area was fully secured by the Moorish forces, Granada grew into an independent city by 1013.

In 1238 Granada became a kingdom, at about the same time the construction of the Alhambra

MOORISH MARKETPLACE

began. The edifice, which in its original and most magnificent form was glistening white in color, was finally completed around 1391. The Muslim rulers lost Granada and the Alhambra in 1492.

By 1800 Granada had become a city of fifteen thousand people. The Old Town of Granada has numerous squares and palaces, and a

RESIDENTIAL BUILDING

narrow market street left over from Muslim times. Many five- and
six-story residential structures were built in the 1800s. I can see
one from my hotel window; it has multiple balconies, some enclosed
with glass, creating solariums, and others with windows covered by
shades that drape over the handrails to block the sun when needed.
All these features add to both the beauty of the building.

STREET ALONG THE DARRO

I continue my walk along the Darro, the Alhambra looming above me on my right and the base of Albaicín on my left. Facing the river are houses and small palaces with their central patios open to the air. On the street side are more solariums and windows with shades draped over the handrails. Most of the houses here were built

SMALL PALACE

between the 1400s and 1600s in the Moorish style, around a central
patio with stairs leading up to the first and second balconies. Many
of the larger buildings are left over from the Moors; these have central patios with finely carved stone columns.

As I leave Granada the next morning, the sight of the Alhambra
brings back Irving's parting words:

CENTRAL PATIO

My serene and happy reign in the Alhambra was sud-
denly brought to a close by letters which reached me, while
indulging in Oriental luxury in the cool hall of the baths,
summoning me away from my Moslem Elysium to mingle
once more in the bustle and business of the dusty world.
How was I to encounter its toils and turmoils, after such a
life of repose and reverie? How was I to endure its common-
place, after the poetry of the Alhambra?[2]

CAMARES BATH ALHAMBRA

The outskirts of Granada have produced new toils and turmoil beyond those Irving could have imagined. The town has grown so much that the old perimeter and its patchwork of agricultural land has been breached, and sprawling development fills the town with noise, air pollution, frantic traffic, and energy demands that combine to create an atmosphere that makes me long, with Irving, for the true poetry of the Alhambra and the human aesthetic sensibilities of the past.

THE PONT-DU-GARD AND VERS

Traveling north up the east coast of Spain through Valencia into Catalonia and Barcelona, I return to France and drive on to Vers, a small village about twelve miles north of Nimes.

This area came under Roman influence in the century before Christ, and Vers got its start as housing for the people working on the Pont-du-Gard, the highest bridge in the Roman world, and on the aqueduct that crosses it. The water flows north from the town of Uzès eight miles to what was the substantial Roman town of Nimes. The village of Vers was built to provide housing for those who worked at a nearby limestone quarry that supplied cut stone for the region and has been in continuous operation to this day.

With its origin as a laborers' village, Vers shows signs of the lack of initial planning. In the center of the village is a small plaza shaded by mature plane trees, with houses facing it on three sides and the back of the church on the fourth. The plaza is the site of festivities, and in the evening one can always find a few people playing the bowling game of *pétanque* or engaged in serious discussion.

Most of the houses are built with outside courtyards. Those with larger courtyards serve as the basis for farming operations beyond the city's edge. The houses are generally two or three stories high, and their courtyards serve both as entrances and a place for animals. The original kitchens and storage rooms, as well as an area for animals, are on the first level. The second level contains the living area and bedrooms, with additional bedrooms on the third level. I am staying in a bedroom on the third level of the home of a friend who moved to Vers several years ago, allowing me a closer look at the home construction here, including the stone foundations, which date back to Roman times.

The houses were built with the same method for masonry construction commonly used throughout Europe. Quarried stone was used for corners, windows, and door frames, while rubble rock was

used for the remaining parts of the walls, which were usually plastered to create a smooth and more durable finish. For important
buildings and those where cost was not a concern, quarried stone
was used throughout. The flooring above the ground level is made of
rectangular limestone slabs that measure approximately twenty
inches long by thirty inches wide by four inches thick and are supported by beams that rest on even thicker girder beams. The roof is
covered with tiles of variegated shades of warm creams and oranges;
most are covered with lichens, adding a whitish cast or, occasionally, a pleasing yellow-orange hue. Surface tiles are laid over a first
course of flat tiles that are supported by wood members lying across
rafter beams. These building techniques appear to have been passed

House with Courtyard

down through the generations and are probably identical to those
used by the Romans when they were here two thousand years ago.

Knowing that parts of these buildings date to Roman times reminds me that houses evolved here just as they have throughout all the towns and villages I have visited, undergoing remodeling over and over again as trends and family needs changed.

Many houses here were remodeled in the 1600s, when making silk was so lucrative that almost every household had a separate room equipped with small fireplaces about three feet up in each corner, where fires were kept burning all winter long to make sure the silk-worms remained alive and healthy. Each family had a silk loom and mul-berry trees in their yards to feed the worms.

In the center of the village, stand-ing under the arch of a most unusual building that in-cludes a clock tower on one side and a house on the other, I look across at a rugged old res-idence that has a simple beauty and wears different ex-pressions, depend-ing on whether its shutters are open or closed. As I look at the surrounding houses, I notice that

NARROW HOUSE ACROSS FROM CHURCH

under the eaves are three courses of inverted tiles, creating a decora-tive supporting ledge between the eave rafters and the wall below. The roofs are low-pitched with gable ends. Throughout the village, decorative carvings embellish doorways, entrances, columns, and chimneys.

HOUSE VIEWED FROM CLOCKTOWER

On the second day of my stay in Vers, my friend offers to show me some of the remains of the Roman aqueduct. During our walk we encounter a cemetery with a small open structure of stone columns

PONT-DU-GARD

supporting a stone roof, some type of shrine. Next to it is an unusual monument with three columns supporting a symbol that I have not seen before and that looks like a sliver moon facing upward with a cross sticking out of it. At first it looks like something that combines Muslim and Christian icons. Then we think it could be the horns of the bull with a sword striking down on them. Martin says the people of this region in France are enthusiastic about bullfighting, and in Vers they celebrate once a year with the running of the bulls. This bit of information gets me wondering, does the icon date back to Roman or earlier times as the symbol of the sacrifice of the bull, or is it simply an expression of the people's fondness for bullfighting?

Without resolution, we continue our walk, reaching sections of the eroding aqueduct. I am amazed that so much effort was exerted two thousand years ago to bring water to a town primarily for affording the luxuries of the public and private baths. After the fall of the Roman Empire, that particular extravagance did not reoccur in Europe until recent times. I am intrigued by this evidence of just how advanced the Roman civilization was.

Finally, we come to the Pont-du-Gard. As I view the series of arches stacked one on top of the other, I am impressed with the skill of the Roman engineers and masons whose feat of engineering carried water across an enormous ravine while maintaining a pleasing aesthetic, the structure contrasting and blending harmoniously with the natural setting. Its visual appeal seems to be produced by the intricacy of the stone construction, which, with the repetition of each course of arches and their diminishing scale, becomes more delicate as the arches move toward the sky. Witnessing the ingenuity and artistry of the Romans, I decide to change my plans once again so I can visit Pompeii in the south of Italy, a Roman city once covered by the ash of a volcanic eruption, and whose remains have gradually been uncovered by archaeologists through the last century.

The next day I bid farewell to my friend and set out for Pompeii in search of further traces of the advanced civilization of the Romans.

IN SEARCH OF THE ROMANS

The journey to Pompeii takes me through Nice, Florence, Rome, and finally to Naples, where I will spend two nights. This schedule allows just one day to see Pompeii, the most revealing of all Roman ruins. In 79 AD Mt. Vesuvius, looming on the city's eastern horizon, erupted, covering the city with volcanic debris, killing those who were not able to escape the gases and hot ash and then preserving it for posterity.

At the time of Pompeii's destruction, the Roman Empire was near the beginning of a monumental expansion that even today continues to hold a remarkable influence on the villages, towns, and cities across Europe. The Roman Republic, with its strong senate, had been transformed into a military dictatorship (the Empire) that still maintained a senate, although with much less power. The stability of the Empire rested more now on its entrenched bureaucracies and well-educated and productive population. But its new energy from strong, opportunistic emperors and their skilled armies spread Roman dominance and culture further around the Mediterranean and through the southern third of Europe.

The growing empire was divided into provinces, each governed by a senator chosen by the emperor. New towns were built in every region to provide the Roman ideals of urban life, in sharp contrast with the existing agrarian lifestyle it was replacing. The towns were laid out in a prescribed grid pattern, with several main streets, and were built with amphitheaters, theaters, basilicas, temples, a forum, and baths. Aqueducts were built to bring water, with underground sewers and water drains to carry the waste away. The architecture was based on Roman and Greek classics but also had regional influences from the local materials and indigenous religious symbols. The Romans' ease at occupying new territory was based in part on their willingness to incorporate local gods and other traditions, and those native peoples who did not resist were treated well and offered opportunities to create an urban life.

With the ash cleared away from Pompeii by careful excavation, the art, architecture, and everyday relics of Roman life are exposed for the world to see. It is on one of Italy's hot, humid July days that I start my walk around the city walls. In Roman times agricultural lands planted in orchards, grains, and vegetables pressed against their edges. I enter the ruins next to the stadium, a large elliptical structure built for watching combat between teams of gladiators from rival towns. Before I look at the inside, curiosity draws me

STADIUM

to an adjacent enclosed field, with arcaded buildings on two sides and a wall around the rest. Archeological evidence shows that, although gladiators practiced here, the field was used primarily for recreation and competition among the younger citizens—running, javelin throwing, gymnastics, and even swimming in a long, narrow pool in the field's center.

Construction of the stadium itself began in 80 BC, about the time Pompeii became a Roman colony, so that Pompeii could participate in regional competition. About twelve years before Pompeii was destroyed, the stadium achieved notoriety when rowdy local fans and their counterparts from a neighboring town got into a brawl, prompting Emperor Nero to close the stadium for a number of years.

It is interesting to hear that some sports fans were so fanatical in support of their gladiators that they would fight among themselves, not much different from the behavior of football and soccer hooligans today.

The town's roots go back to the seventh century BC, when the indigenous Italic people began to build houses here, at the intersection of three main roads. Pompeii's favorable position next to the coast allowed the development of a port, which was key to its sustained growth through the years. The town soon fell under the influence of the Greeks, whose power and culture were spreading rapidly. In the sixth century BC the Etruscans, who came from the area north of Rome and extended as far as Bologna, brought advanced building technologies that appear to have influenced engineering and building throughout southern Italy.

Like other Roman towns, Pompeii had inherited much of its culture, architecture, civil engineering, science, philosophy, and religion from the Greeks and the Etruscans. Around 310 BC Roman influences, which had began to overpower the Greeks, reached Pompeii. I begin to wonder how the rural, agrarian Romans were ultimately able to dominate their parent cultures, expand through the Mediterranean, Western Asia, and much of Europe and produce what many consider to be the greatest and most advanced civilization up to that time. Certainly the Romans developed a powerful army, but that alone could not have ensured their success. Perhaps it was education. The Roman equivalents of primary, secondary, and high-school programs effectively educated a large percentage of the population, creating opportunities for its citizens in its towns and cities as well as in the conquered territories. In Pompeii, classes for primary and secondary education were held in the shelter of the porticoes around the Forum or in other public places, while high schools and most trade school classes took place in a teacher's house or shop. Although the wealthiest could afford to hire private tutors to come into their homes, any Roman citizen could send his children, whether male or female, to school. Men could continue to whatever level their aptitude and family finances would allow. While a class system existed and many students were directed to trade schools, almost anyone displaying ability and desire could work his way up the ladder to become a surveyor, engineer, architect, lawyer, doctor, or banker. For the most part, however, upper-class Romans chose careers in the military, politics, or finance; the middle class took jobs in architecture or medicine; and poorer citizens became crafts-men, teachers, or shopkeepers. Most slaves took up manual work such as building and mining, although some of them had comfortable jobs as teachers or servants or in financial affairs. Having this broad spectrum of educated people, including resident Greeks and Greek slaves, provided both the personnel required to operate Rome's well-organized economy and governing bureaucracy and the intellectual skills to understand and respect the necessity to abide by the Roman system of rules and laws.

PORTICO AT ATHLETIC FIELD

As I leave the field in Pompeii's stadium, I feel the energy of the young runners and javelin throwers who practiced and competed here over two thousand years ago, and for a moment I can visual-ize men in their white tunics and women in subtly colored stolas standing in the shade of the surrounding porticoes, watching their children compete.

Walking north one block and turning left onto one of Pompeii's major streets, I can see nearly a mile to the other end of town. The street's cobbles are deeply rutted with parallel tracks from hundreds of years of use by chariots and carts. Raised sidewalks on each side are paved with flat stones, or, in special locations, such as in front of a temple or baths, with marble. Every fifty to one hundred feet or so, I pass some raised stones in the street that would have required a chariot to slow down to a walking pace—an early version of speed control, or perhaps a pedestrian crossing. Here and there I notice

MAIN STREET

rectangular water basins with fresh water coming from a spout in the shape of an animal head. They must have been used as a drinking fountain or for animals, since running water was piped to the inside of the buildings. The underground sewer system carries waste from the streets and some of the public buildings with pulses of flowing water, remaining out of sight below the street's surface. With the demise of the Roman Empire and the destruction of its towns and cities, this level of convenience and sanitation was lost for fifteen hundred years.

SIDE STREET

Narrow side streets extend from the main road in each direction. Pompeii's gridded street layout was based on the Greek concept of town planning, which was adopted by the Romans and became a trademark of the new towns built during their reign.

The houses on the east side of the street generally have only one level, while those on the west usually have two, most likely in an effort to provide afternoon shade on the street and sidewalks during the heat of late day. For hundreds of years these streets would have been quite busy, especially early in the morning and at noontime,

ATRIUM

when people generally took their meals at the cafés rather than at home, as they did in the evening. As I pass shops, bakeries, and cafés, I notice marble counters built right to the edge of the sidewalk for serving those standing outside.

Houses, most built several hundred years before Christ, range in size from small residences that have no outside space to villas that have large gardens overlooked by rooms with porticoes. The homes and villas almost always have an atrium entrance—a room with an opening in the roof and a rectangular pool of water directly under the opening—and there were rooms used for conducting business, entertaining, dining, cooking, sleeping, storing goods, bathing, and a latrine.

Inside I can see the decorative styles popular at the time of Pompeii's demise. The floors are covered with intricate mosaics of geometric patterns, animals, human figures, and scenic vignettes, the most elaborate among them appearing in the atria. The walls are viv-

WALL PAINTING

idly colored, with predominating shades of diluted reds and gold. Many of the walls are covered with frescoes, murals, or paintings, revealing a remarkable level of talent by the city's artisans. The rich texture and color of floor mosaics and the delicately painted walls with scenes depicting important myths, events, gods, erotic encounters, animals, and symbols enriched the residents' daily routines and displayed for visitors their interests and values. I can imagine a special dinner party planned just for the purpose of unveiling a new wall painting.

Construction is of rock and brick walls with a plastered coat-
ing to create a smooth surface. Carved stone decorates the arches or
lintels over doorways. Thick, round, or square columns, occasionally
fluted, support stone lintel beams around porticoes. The roofs are
built with timber rafters and topped by the standard Roman roof
tiles, with a flat piece curling up on the sides to contain rainwater
and a curved cap tile covering the seams where the flat tiles abut
each other.

Farther up the street I reach the forum, a large rectangular open
space once used for markets, trade, civic functions, and formal and
informal social and political events. The forum was the center of all
Roman towns and cities and the predecessor of the piazza, plaza,
and town square. On the edges of the forum are a number of temples,
a basilica, a market building, and a large public building used for
courts of law and municipal offices. Near the forum are two theaters,

OUTDOOR THEATER

a large outdoor theater built under Greek influence in the second
century BC, which was used for a variety of performances, and a
smaller indoor one built around 75 BC for concerts and dramas.

Temples and other public buildings were made with the same
techniques as houses but have more exposed decorative stonework
and are more open and airy, with outside courts and gardens. The

public baths, on the other hand, have more of an enclosed feeling, with soft, filtered light from small roof openings finding its way into the assortment of rooms, creating an effect similar to that which I found in several rooms at the Alhambra. The effects of light must have been similar inside the most ancient houses as well. They did not have windows but allowed the natural light to filter in through small roof openings, dimly illuminating the interior spaces.

BATHS

Buildings in Pompeii extend to the property line, so windows—usually with iron bars for security—face only the street in front or the gardens in the rear. The same pattern in somewhat modified form existed in Arcos de la Frontera. According to archaeologists, this building layout can be traced back to towns found in Mesopotamia dating to 5000 BC, when buildings were placed back-to-back and abutted on their sides, with the only light coming from the roof or internal courts. In Mesopotamia the buildings were built with mud bricks and timbers supporting the roofs. From the sixth century BC in the Mediterranean area, urn-fired clay and mud-brick construction was giving way to stronger, more permanent kiln-fired brick construction (which, in combination with stone, was the material of choice for building). At that time, builders also discovered that a stronger and more permanent mortar could be made from volcanic ash or lime from kiln-fired crushed limestone. I can see evidence in Pompeii of these techniques that spread through the world and are still used today.

INDOOR SHRINE

The columns used in temples and basilicas and the supporting porticoes on public buildings and around the gardens on private houses must surely have been seen by the residents as among the noblest features, with the massive forms symbolizing strength and power. The use of vivid color inside and out of the houses must have been important as well, a contrast with other places that are more monochromatic or white and accented only by wood or stone. The atrium would have been another essential symbol for every household, with larger houses having multiple atria, usually located just through an entrance vestibule. The naturally lit space with a view to the sky ties the house to the heavens, while the symbol of water at the base connects it to the earth. Gardens were also important in the houses, villas, and temples. They were a visual extravagance—a place to meditate or just to view and spend time enjoying the flowers, shrubs, pools, fountains, and sculpture.

Sculptures of heroes or gods distinguished both public and private spaces, indicating their special and symbolic importance. Religious altars or shrines for prayer or meditation were common in the household, creating a constant visual reminder of the perceived spiritual world. As I sit on the front steps of the Temple of Apollo, which dates back to 550 BC, and stare across the Forum at the Temple of Vespasian, I see an altar with a scene depicting the sacrifice of a bull. I think back to Vers and the symbol I saw there, possibly, of the killing of the bull, and I wonder whether the bullfight in Christian cultures has descended from Pagan-Roman bull sacrifices.

Enjoying my resting spot, I take the time to read more about the Roman educational system. I run across a Roman boy's description of a typical day at school from ancient papers that were part of an archaeological discovery from the period just after the birth of Christ:

> I awoke in the morning and was handed a towel and water to wash myself. I put on a tunic and belt and combed and scented my hair. I put on a cloak and wrapped a scarf around my neck and left my room to say good morning to my mother and father. I kissed them goodbye and was accompanied to school by family servants. I stopped at a bakery that is well stocked with sweets. I met up with my friends as I arrived at school and started the morning lessons. I came home for lunch and had white bread, olives, cheese, dried figs and walnuts and fresh water. I went back to school and continued with Latin and Greek language lessons. After asking to be excused at the end of the session, I left school and headed to the baths with some friends before returning home for the evening.[3]

These words from a young boy indicate that there was a strong air of politeness and civility among the populace, which is certainly in keeping with the formality and orderliness of the architecture. As I head back to my hotel I see more evidence of how civilized and advanced the Romans were as indicated by the boy's writing. I think back to my first glimpse of the Pont-du-Gard aqueduct in France, which had once carried water to the town of Nimes. My assumption then was that the water was mainly for hygiene, sanitation, and drinking. Now, seeing Pompeii and reading this schoolboy's words, I am coming to see the importance of Roman baths for improved health and relaxation. In fact, everything I see here leads me to believe the inhabitants of Roman towns were more highly civilized than has been depicted in our movies and literature, which have accentuated the bizarre and violent parts of Roman culture and left people with what I believe is a mistaken impression.

I leave Pompeii seeing many similarities between Roman civilization and our own. What can we learn from them? There are still parts of the world today shows few signs of being more humanely civilized, and the totality of their architecture was aesthetically superior to what we all have to look at today.

CORTONA

From Pompeii I head north to Cortona. Perched on a mountain-side high above the Chiana Valley in central Tuscany, the town embodies the true spirit, history, and meaning of a city-state. From the time of its early Ligurian inhabitants ten thousand years ago, the indigenous people here have maintained a high degree of autonomy. They accommodated the resident Umbrians, who migrated either from central Europe or from the Balkans, as well as the Etruscans, upon whose culture and early foundations the existing city walls rest, and they resisted and avoided domination by the Romans, Goths, Carolingians, and Saracens. Cortona had intermittent skirmishes and alliances with its many city-state neighbors over control of the

CORTONA

rich farmland in the valley below, the grazing land on the slopes of the Apennine Mountains, and the surrounding hills that hold rich, usable sandstone, timber, copper, iron, and other minerals.

I enter the town through its lower gate and walk up a steep street to my hotel. That evening, as I enjoy supper in the dining room on the first floor, I gaze at the ceiling construction and beam work

STEEP STREET

and notice its similarity to what I saw in Vers. As I am served pick-
led vegetables, pasta with a white sauce covered with thinly sliced
white truffles, and a glass of the local white wine, I delight again in
the change in food, which has reflected each unique culture as much
as the architecture has.

After dinner I read that foundations of circular buildings built
by the early Umbrians in 800 BC have been discovered in the area.

DINNING ROOM

Historical records show that the early Etruscan development here was occurring parallel to that of the Greeks who colonized the Southern Coastal area of Italy. Some think the Etruscans may have moved out of the Middle East; others believe they may have been the local people influenced by the Phoenicians and Syrians around 800 BC. The spiral symbol found on an Etruscan tomb, also heavily used in the Celtic culture and still used in Cortona today, may indicate common roots between the Celts and Etruscans or may, because of its simplicity, be an independent invention that was used in many cultures.

I recall the detailing on a window I passed on my way into town, with its carved stone ledge and supports, and wonder whether it might have been influenced by symbols from the Etruscans, Celts, or Romans. Cortona underwent continual changes through the centuries, but the early roads that traverse the steep slopes and most of the protective walls have remained. Cortona eventually became part of the Roman Empire, with full citizenship for its inhabitants in 67 BC, but the town retained more of its autonomy than many others. The main evidence of the Roman presence is the remains of three baths.

CARVED STONE LEDGE

During the first two hundred years after the collapse of the Roman Empire, Cortona gradually became impoverished. In the mid-500s AD, the Goths and Lombards attacked the towns of this region but chose to build their own castles apart from the cities, creating many small dukedoms. During this time the Catholic Church was striving to take control, with bishops heading some of the defunct Roman towns. In the 770s AD, King Charlemagne of France conquered the Lombards and restored a semblance of order by dividing the country into counties to be administered by counts or magnates. This arrangement still left the town without much power, but by the 1000s and 1100s Cortona—like most towns under French authority at the time—had regained self-rule, and by 1200 the town was flourishing, with many new buildings and a thriving population. People had begun fleeing the feudal estates of the counts and the magnates in order to reside within the protective walls of the city. With growing military might, Cortona forced the surrounding counts to submit to the city's jurisdiction, setting up the relationship it has today with its surrounding small villages, where the people consider themselves Cortonians.

I begin my exploration of Cortona the next day. Many of the buildings are made of sandstone, though some of the very oldest,

ELEVENTH-CENTURY HOUSES

dating to the 1000s, are half-timbered with brick masonry supported by wood knee-bracing over-hanging the street at the second level. Many of the build-ings are plastered and painted with a pal-ette of yellows and light crimson colors, similar to those used in Pompeii. With the exception of the fa-cades of the buildings, which underwent various changes rep-resenting Baroque and Renaissance design, the building patterns along the streets of Cortona were set in place between 1000 and 1200 AD. Governmental and church buildings of quarried stone in varying architectural styles lie on the main road and around the two main plazas. At one point, I climb a broad set of steps, nearly twenty feet high, to the doors of the city's main municipal govern-ment building. Across the way a street emerges from the plaza and

then switches back above it, creating an upper terrace partially covered by an arcade. Numerous balconies on the remaining buildings
add to the available vantage points overlooking the plaza. On my last
night in town I am fortunate to attend a concert and witness how
the plaza can become an accidental theater.

The individual buildings are all interesting but present a somewhat awkward blend. The visual discomfort is overcome, however,
by the activity on the balconies, in the windows, and in the numer-

PIAZZA

ous shops, and from the energy created by the accumulation of people from the five streets that converge at this one point.

As I look down from the elevated walkway overlooking all the
activities, I realize that this plaza and other similar gathering places
take on a special symbolic meaning because of the entertainment
that they afford. This is where we have fun, these places seem to
say; this is where people come to add joy and pleasure to their lives.
Theaters, baths, circuses, greens, piazzas, parks, pubs, and cafés all
share this symbolic meaning. They and their symbols elicit feelings
ranging from relaxation to excitement, and they provide a broader
sense of community, where our interactions with others spark emotions that help satisfy our social needs. As important as these places

are to the quality of our lives and their historical presence in our communities, they are absent from many of today's architectural settings.

As I walk along one of the streets leading from the plaza, I notice that some of the shops have stone ledges protruding into the street, similar to those I saw in Dinan, France. I remember that shops in

Pompeii had similar counters extending to the street for the sale of their quick snacks or meals. Once again I see the importance of Rome as the source of what has been built in Europe through the years.

Cortona has a rich diversity of houses, in both size and style. Through the years interiors have been remodeled to keep up with new inventions and trends in

SERVING COUNTER

design, but the houses still express character based on their medieval roots. The roofs are all of red-orange tiles—many aged and turning white with lichens and bird droppings—and exhibit the Roman villa patterns of flat tiles, with inverted curved tiles covering the seams.

Small plazas are abundant in the town. Two of them overlook the lands below: one to the west in front of St. Margaret Church and the others to the south. Within the walls of the town on the upper end is a substantial area for vegetable gardens and fruit trees. Figs, apricots, vines, vegetables, and kumquats grow in people's individual yards. Terraced trees and crops, interspersed with wooded areas, surround the outside walls in every direction.

ROMAN ROOF TILES AND CHIMNEYS

Nine gates surround Cortona, with the roads converging at the two major plazas. An occasional narrow pedestrian passage connects one street to the next. The buildings face the street on one side and, on the other side, a planted open area in the center of the block allows light to come from both front and back. Balconies can be seen on both sides, and some of the grander houses have terraced gardens next to the street.

As I walk the narrow streets and even narrower footpaths, I find a surprise around every turn: a little plaza, a house with an unusual but attractive design, a view across the village walls of the countryside. A glimpse into the houses offers additional interesting views—beam ceilings supporting red tiles, unique fireplace designs, and windows looking into gardens or across the Chiana Valley.

TERRACED GARDENS

As I leave Cortona and think back to the special beauty of each town with its variations in architectural design, I find myself appreciating the layers of culture that lie beneath—here in Italy, those of the Etruscans and the Romans, and in Spain, of the more exotic Moors—all with their influence coloring the present, much like a genetic imprint reflecting in us the traits of our ancestors.

ASSISI

Assisi

Backtracking a bit to the southeast to get to my next destination, I make my way through a vast region of fertile agricultural lands, around the eastern shore of Lake Trasimeno, and then through the city-state of Perugia, a past rival of both Cortona and Assisi, before catching my first glimpse of Assisi through an olive orchard. The impressively large white band on the mountainside directly in front of me looks like a crown, with the St. Francis Basilica and surrounding convent prominent in the foreground like a centerpiece. Unlike Sare in the Basque region of France or Arcos de la Frontera in Andalusia, Assisi does not appear pure white but is rather a blend of cream- and light brown-colored limestone buildings. The town is surrounded by orchards of olive and fruit trees, vineyards and pastures, and stands of small straggly hardwoods.

Assisi's Umbrian inhabitants date back to Stone Age times. There is evidence of religious ceremonies being held here as early as 5000 BC. Archaeological findings and historical documents also reveal in subsequent years a tradition of devotion to many divinities: Hercules, Aretei, Bonus Eventus Ianipoter, Jupiter, Pagonicus, Minerva, and the Dioscuri Castor and Pollux. It is interesting that Assisi's early development was spurred in part by its importance as a religious gathering place, as Assisi later became famous as the home of St. Francis—known for his reverence toward nature and his concerns about the trappings of material wealth.

BASILICA OF ST. FRANCIS

In the centuries preceding the birth of Christ, the town grew under the influence of neighboring Perugia, a powerful and prosperous Etruscan city, until 295 BC, when Assisi fell under Roman influence, eventually becoming part of the Roman confederation in 89 BC. At that time Assisi had a forum, baths, amphitheaters, and a circus. After the fall of the Roman Empire the town was damaged by invaders, occupied first by the Lombards and then by Charlemagne's armies, who destroyed the town's protective walls. In the 1000s, with the help of the Church, Assisi initiated significant reconstruction, and a period of prosperity began. In the centuries leading to the 1800s, however, its economy and civic achievements fell victim to constant feuding among the leading families. Nevertheless, Assisi kept its independent status until the mid-1800s, when it agreed to became part of the Italian Federation.

As I enter the lower main gate, I immediately notice that the buildings have more of an ancient character than any I've seen so far. I find a room in a house that has been converted to a hotel for people on pilgrimage. The hotel owner says times are good here because of the number of people coming to see the homes of St. Francis and St. Clare and the Basilica of St. Francis.

I spend the early part of my second day walking along the streets looking at houses. After a noon meal, I make my way to the St. Francis Basilica. The soft, creamy-white stone edifice stands above a piazza surrounded by a continuous portico. As I enter the church, I feel immediately the same dominating and awe-inspiring presence I felt in the shadows of the church at Santillana del Mar, Spain, and my simulated trip into the depths of the Altamira Cave. I make my way through the dark, following the nave to my left, which slopes down to the presbytery and altar. A flickering light from the banks of candles on the tables shimmers warmly on the vaulted ceiling. On close inspection, I see that the arched supports of the vaults are painted with intricate ribbons of geometric and floral patterns. Eloquent paintings of saints and biblical stories are brought to life by the strobe of candlelight reflecting off the walls and vaults. I sit in a pew for a while, struck by the power of the arched vaults and the indescribable feeling of mystery arising from all I see.

Unaware of how long I have rested here, I get up and walk to a steep stone stairway that leads down to the tomb of St. Francis. The small crypt is lit by hundreds of candles, and as I walk around it I feel a chill start at the back of my head and travel through my body. A lump forms in my throat and tears run down my cheeks. I am

BASILICA OF ST FRANCIS

taken completely by surprise by my response; I am not a particularly religious person in the conventional sense, though as a young boy I occasionally attended church services. I stand there for a few minutes and collect myself, then make my way up the stairs and slowly through the basilica to the door and the piazza.

Outside it is bright, and I am not really ready to move on. I back into the basilica for a moment, curious about what I have just felt. While I relate to Christ's powerful message of selfless service to others, which I find essential to human happiness and survival, my experience with organized religion has been that this message is too often misrepresented or lost.

It occurs to me now that perhaps something about this space and my frame of mind have allowed me to connect in some way with St. Francis and his values, which I find admirable and inspiring. I wonder whether this kind of experience is why so many people make pilgrimages to the town of St. Francis, or for that matter to other sacred shrines, whether Buddhist, Muslim, Jewish, or Hindu. My experience helps me to better understand the significance of religious symbols and how churches, temples, and the multitude of icons depicting gods, saints, and devotional objects can evoke feelings both meaningful and intense for those who make a connection. I also realize that each individual interprets these experiences based on beliefs developed during childhood and throughout life.

After a few moments I am finally able to walk back outside and head to the Piazza del Comune, which is located on a long terrace in the center of this hillside town. This was the site of the early Etruscan marketplace several hundred years before Roman occupation. The ancient stone paving now lies buried below the existing piazza. The piazza is still surrounded by medieval buildings and the Roman Temple of Minerva, which, built in the first century BC, is at least thirteen hundred years older than the rest. As I look around the piazza I try to imagine how different it was when the Romans were here and how much it has changed. The Temple of Minerva feels ancient, but not so much that it seems totally out of place.

While walking to my hotel I spot the entrance to a city museum and enter through an underground tunnel, which is part of the crypt of St. Nicolo. Standing now on original Roman stone paving below

GRAVE MARKER

the piazza, I can see numerous artifacts as well as grave and tomb markers laid against early stonework, forming the walls of the tomb. On a wall is a dimly lit map of unknown origin, depicting the Roman town that once stood here with its forum predating the piazza through which I just walked. How many Roman towns, I wonder, were as magnificent as the one in this drawing? As I look carefully at the map I can see that Assisi today is laid out similarly to the Roman town that existed here sixteen centuries ago, its streets following the same ancient pattern.

ROMAN ASSISI

Leaving the underground tomb, I continue on my way, carefully examining each building, noting the unique expression or vision

WINDOWS AND STONE LEDGE

of the architects and original owners. I come across a wedge-shaped house that is thought to have been the headquarters of the skilled Lombard masons, who worked in Assisi to build the Basilica and the convent of St. Francis. On the walls, carved in stone, are the symbols of the master bricklayers: a compass, a five-petal rose, a mallet, and a T-square.

That night at supper I ask my server more about St. Francis. I learn that the saint was born here in 1181 to a prosperous merchant

HOME OF THE MASTER MASONS

family. He grew up with the dream of becoming a knight and leading a life of military achievement. Over time he grew disillusioned with

FOURTEENTH-CENTURY HOUSE

such worldly successes and dedicated himself to works of charity. His life's work and the religious order he established were intended to emphasize that real wealth was found not in material things but in relation to the beauties of nature and in the simple acts of growing and preparing food, building, and nurturing quality relationships with others. St. Clare likewise left a wealthy family to follow her friend, and shortly before her death founded the religious order known as the Poor Clares in order to promote in perpetuity St. Francis's ideals.

BELLS OF THE CHURCH OF SANTO STEFANO

During a late-evening walk on my last night in Assisi, I ponder the changes the town has seen and what remains—from a site for pagan religious ceremonies to an Etruscan and later a Roman settlement, from a prosperous medieval city to a town most remembered today as the home of St. Francis and St. Clare. I turn a corner to see yet another image of the town cast by the silhouette of the three bells on the Church of Santo Stefano, a parting image from the builders of Assisi whose influence has been felt in Christian Architecture around the world.

RADOVLJICA

Radovljica

A day's travel brings me to the border crossing between Italy and Slovenia, moving from what in the 1850s would have been the Italic Papal States to the province of Carniola in the Austrian Empire. My destination, Radovljica, lies at the southern end of the Alps. Due to its location at a crossroads, with Europe to the west, Asia to the east, the Balkans to the south, and the Alps and Germanic plain to the north, the region's politics and ethnic composition have changed frequently through the centuries. Here on the edge of what had once been the Roman Empire, the Goths used the region for staging attacks on the Romans. The Romans, however, prevailed and expanded their settlements throughout the region as they moved northward. In the 600s AD the area became the home of Slavic people, who settled here to escape the Huns, who had invaded their homeland to the north. Within a hundred years or so, however, the Slavic dukedom was subsumed by Charlemagne under the Frankish Empire. Soon after, under the influence of Charlemagne, the people here converted to Christianity.

As I make my way up the Sava River I can see that the plateaus above are covered with fields of grain separated by deep, lush forests. Lying on one of these plateaus, Radovljica became a modest market town in the 1300s but later grew in importance because of its proximity to iron mines and to bountiful farms, which have spurred the growth of a population that has forced the town's boundaries beyond its medieval walls.

TOWN CENTER

The town is built around a long central plaza, bordered by government buildings and the houses of nobles and merchants. A church, established in the 1100s, sits at the south end, where a market is held weekly.

Church of St. Peter

The simple stone houses are of a character I have not seen so far. Referred to here as burgher houses, most were built in the 1400s and 1500s. Some have vaulted ceilings over the ground floor, occasionally with the vaults extending over the lower wall, allowing the upper levels to hang over the street. Some are painted with classical columns and decorations, and others with pictures on the plaster or bas-relief. I wonder about the origins of the term *burgher house*. Does it refer to a style or a time period? I note it has similarities to the Baroque style.

At several museums I am drawn to the remarkable artistry of food presentation. The silverware, dishware, and glassware, along with the beautiful hand-carved furniture and woven linens from the

BURGHER HOUSES

past, are highly refined with intricate detail, each an individual, one-of-a-kind piece of art. My attention to architecture, up to this point, has distracted me from noticing the rich variations in the other objects in people's lives back then, such as the housewares and furnishings that today I am finally paying attention to. A museum display prompts me to imagine what it would have been like to attend a dinner here 150 years ago. I can see the food, each course appearing in a colorful presentation that includes glazed and decorated bread rolls that have been arranged next to a plate of burgundy-colored gelatin, cast in a mold leaving a relief of a village scene. In homage to the region's renown for beekeeping, the dessert has a highly intricate pattern of crystallized honey, making each serving look as though it has been etched individually.

I spend the next day in the surrounding area, traveling from hamlet to hamlet in the hills to the north and finishing in Bled, a village on a pristine lake with a castle and several villas overlooking its calm, deep-blue water. The hamlets, each with its own church of unique character, are so close together that sometimes I can see as many as five steeples from one location. The hamlets are composed

VILLAGE CHURCH

of fifteen to forty farmhouses, with barns sometimes attached and sometimes separate. Each barn is adorned with intricately decorated wood detailing. Open sheds provide storage for farm equipment and are lined on several sides with horizontal wood rails for drying and storing hay. The houses, barns, and sheds all have moderately pitched roofs covered with wood shingles that have semicircular bottom edges. Each home has a neatly cultivated vegetable garden and fruit trees.

These hamlets appear quite self-sufficient, and, based on the architecture, seem to be made up of an egalitarian class of inhabitants. The small white churches, most on the edges of the villages but some set a short distance away, are surrounded by low walls that enclose

VILLAGE CHURCH

cemeteries. Each one also has an open-sided covered vestibule in front in which people can gather prior to entering the church. The steeples on the churches vary, with some narrow and tapered to the top and others with a bulge that reveals a Byzantine influence.

For more than an hour on this warm summer day, I wander around the lake at Bled. In at least five different places, I see children swimming and playing in the water. Occasionally I walk past one or two men sitting on a log, fishing poles in hand. I can see large fish swimming in the crystal-clear water, paying little attention to the fishermen's bait. As I continue along, I realize what a luxury it is to live on or close to water. It is a source of recreation and the aquatic life a source of food, but the presence of a lake, river, or ocean also provides a vantage point for expansive and uninterrupted views of natural beauty, similar in many ways to those seen from the heights of hills or mountains, such as I experienced at the bastide Domme.

HOUSE AND BARN

These hamlets scattered through the hills, with the Alps rising above them to the north, exude an air of wholesomeness and peace. They are places of pristine and delicate beauty, so untroubled now, even though for centuries they have lain in the midst of war and strife. As I leave, enjoying my last views of the villages, I see hints of the distinct but highly varied style of architecture that extends through the Alps.

KASTELRUTH

Heading back into Italy I make my way up the south slopes of the Tyrolean Alps, past Bolzano-Bozen. I follow a river gorge with steep mountains on each side that occasionally open into little valleys. I see small villages and vineyards along the slopes in places where the grade allows for building and cultivation. High on the side of the mountains, amid the dark-green forest, I see pastures and farmhouses where the trees have been cleared. Well into the Tyrolean Alps now, I am getting close to the mountain town of Kastelruth.

After traversing a number of switchbacks in a steep-sided tributary of the river, I finally reach the upper plateau, the Schlern, as it is called, surrounded by the high limestone peaks of the Siusi Alps. There are wooded glens, alpine meadows, and at least nine villages,

ALPINE BARN

SIUSI ALPS

all surrounded by numerous farms. As I pass by one of the farms, I notice the unique wood design that the builder had detailed on the barn.

KASTELRUTH

As I get close to Kastelruth I can see its tall bell tower. On arrival, I walk up the hill behind the village center, past several small,
open chapels, to get a bird's-eye view of town. A prehistoric fortress
once stood here, destroyed during the Roman invasion and replaced

by a Roman fortification about 15 BC. The remains of round stone huts that archeologists date back to at least 5000 BC were found just beyond the outer walls of where the old fortress stood, not far from where I stand.

The well-preserved remains of one ancient hunter—Otzi, as he is called locally—were discovered not far from here; archeologists believe he came from a time five or six thousand years ago. He was found falling out of the edge of a melting glacier with clothing, a

flint dagger with an ash handle inside a sheath of woven grasses, an ax with a copper blade and a handle of yew wood, a bow and leather quiver with fourteen arrows, and a variety of home possessions still intact. He had been frozen in time until 1991, when the melting ice exposed his remains. It is likely that Otzi lived in one of the prehistoric round huts in one of the early settlements around here and came

CHAPEL

to misfortune on a trip away from his home. Early human presence at such a high elevation and in such a harsh winter climate indicates that even six or seven thousand years ago the expanding population in Europe was so large that some people were pushed to, or even chose, the frontier of the high mountains.

The placing of the round houses close to a fortress changed eventually as people's sense of safety increased, to dispersed sites that could more easily be farmed, making them the predecessors of the isolated farmsteads I see across the foothills around Kastelruth.

STREET TO PIAZZA

I walk back down to the village through two narrow streets. Each has a building with a corner turret producing an intriguing

CONVENT

vista termination. The turrets create visual drama from the street
and provide unique viewing opportunities from the inside. I enter

the market square, where a large spring-fed fountain once supplied water for the townspeople. The village center consists of a hotel, a municipal building that from 1550 to 1800 served as the palace of the ruling Kraus family, and a convent, all surrounding piazza Kraus.

PIAZZA KRAUS

The buildings, which date back as far as the 1400s, were built with stone and then plastered and whitewashed. From a distance they are simple in appearance, but at close range they display fine woodwork on and around the doors and windows, adding intricacy to their uncomplicated beauty. Some of the windows are shuttered, while others, especially in the oldest buildings, are not. As I walk around I notice an unusual abstract pattern of windows on the convent that creates an irregular but balanced composition. I wonder whether the pattern is intentional or simply the result of the lighting needs inside the building.

In the evening, I wander up the hills among the pastures and farmhouses. It is balmy and comfortable, but I know that's an exception here in Kastelruth, where the temperatures can be so extreme. What moved people to venture into this remote region so long ago? Were they moving away from an expanding population to find new resources where there was no competition ? Or were they people

CONVENT

whose Ice Age ancestry led them to prefer this kind of climate? Would the pure splendor of the natural beauty have been enough to draw them and to keep them here through the harsh winters? Ruskin came to the Alps in the 1800s to sketch the mountain peaks, crags, and valleys. His wonder at their grandeur, as well as my own experience of awe in their presence, makes me believe something within us reacts to their sight. Even though I know the ability to obtain or grow food would be a greater motivation, maybe the power of the massive limestone peaks rising above the trees and meadows was enough then to hold people in this place through the severe winters.

HALLSTATT

HALLSTATT

I leave Italy and drive into Austria, continuing to notice the variations in alpine architecture. When I arrive at the north end of Hallstatt Lake, the daylight is almost gone. One hundred and fifty years ago I would have had to wait until the next morning to catch a ride across the lake on a gondola or rowboat. A narrow trail around the lake provided the only other access.

The next morning, as the sun is just beginning to rise, I rent a boat and row out into the lake to capture a view of the town. As the sun climbs the steep western slope of the lake, I see the reflections of Hallstatt marred only slightly by the rippling of the water's surface from the light morning breeze. To me, the view, with its timbered boathouse

WATERFRONT HOUSES AND CATHOLIC CHURCH

at the water's edge and a landscape of roofs pitched in different directions rising above, as well as the two churches with their larger forms, completes a composition that remains perfect regardless of vantage point. This is the prettiest of all the villages and towns I have seen on my journey.

From the dock it is a short distance to a small triangular marketplace, which 150 years ago would have been crowded with people buying and selling meat, vegetables, grains, and furnishings. Salt merchants would have been negotiating with their customers, and caged chickens would have made a fuss, only to be drowned out by the clatter of donkey carts pulling their load of goods over the cobbles. I sit down at a table and order the same breakfast of bread, wurst, and dark beer that would have been served here over a century ago.

MARKET SQUARE

In late morning the bright sun gives way to a light rain, a typical weather pattern here. I walk through the rain and visit both Catholic and Protestant churches. During the Reformation, the rebellion against the Catholic Church was stronger in Hallstatt because workers in the salt industry felt exploited by the Catholic-influenced government, which sanctioned low wages and harsh working conditions, while the new Protestant religion was promising better wages and conditions. The movement was so strong here that even during the Counter-Reformation, the Protestant Church could not be driven out of Hallstatt.

MOUNTAINSIDE HOUSES

One road near the shoreline meanders between buildings and the lake. Walking toward the market square, I see a building serving as a guest house that has a turret like those I saw in Kastelruth. Like the others, it creates an intriguing composition when viewed look-ing down the narrow street. The masonry buildings here are similar

STREET TO MARKET SQUARE

to those in Kastelruth and Radovljica, and the wood-framed buildings are similar to the Swiss alpine cottages to the west. Houses on
the mountainside are accessible only by footpath.

The second day, after a steep forty-five-minute climb above the
lake, I take a tour of the salt mine, the town's economic mainstay
since ancient times. I am guided by the written narratives from both

a local museum and Johann Georg Ramsauer, who directed mining operations in the mid-1800s and who discovered an ancient Celtic cemetery that dates back to 700 BC. According to Ramsauer, there is some indication that early salt mining occurred in Stone Age times, more than six thousand years ago. Large-scale mining of salt deposits seems to have started around 1400 BC and continues to this day, likely making Hallstatt the oldest salt mine in the world. In 200 BC the first contacts took place between the local Celts of the Norikum Kingdom and the Roman Empire. With the Romans expanding northward, the Celts were becoming direct neighbors and sought ways to live in peace, a definite advantage over war, since the Romans made valuable trading partners. The people here depended on the export of salt and the trade and traffic it brought. In 15 BC the situation for the Norikum Kingdom changed dramatically under the superpower ambitions of the Roman Emperor Augustus. The Romans took over by sending an occupying force to Hallstatt to take up residence. Local historians assume that the Romans took over all positions of power as well as control over the salt mine. The Celts had built their settlements high on the mountain near the salt mine, but the Romans preferred the edge of the lake, where Hallstatt exists today. They lived in lavishly furnished villas with under-floor heating and glass windows, evidence of their advanced technology.

After my tour of the mine and a look at the Celtic archaeological excavations, I hike back down to the lake. As darkness falls in the shadow of the mountains, I sit down for a trout dinner and a glass of Riesling, and then head up to my room on the old stone building's third floor, which has a wood balcony overlooking the lake. As I gaze out on the lake's moonlit surface with the mountains visible in the distance, I know I am fortunate to have this opportunity to feel the magnificent beauty that all those who have lived here through the centuries experienced, from the early natives to the Celts, Romans, and the people who came after.

EGER

I head next for Hungary, my most easterly destination. Traveling northeast from Hallstatt, I have to make my way down out of the mountains onto the great Pannonian Plain, through Vienna, then across farmland to Budapest.

I arrive in Buda, which, along with the old town of Pest, straddles the Danube River. They combined in 1873 to form the capital city today known as Budapest. I settle into my hotel and then go for a dip in the city's famous Turkish baths. The elegant baths continue as a remnant of the Turkish occupation of the Ottoman Empire, which began around 1541 AD and lasted for about 150 years. The baths descended from the Byzantines, the Romans, and before that the Greeks; but through time and from country to country have gradually undergone considerable evolution in architecture. Soaking in them provides me the closest experience to the kind of luxury that existed in Rome and Greece over two thousand years ago. I wonder how such a tradition of luxury could have continued in the Turkish culture on the fringe of Europe when, after the fall of Rome, through the Middle Ages, and until the twentieth century, bathing was exceedingly infrequent for the rest of the people in Europe.

After one of my soundest night's sleep and a breakfast of eggs and bacon, I go directly to the Magyar Törtenelmi Muzeum to learn as much about Hungary as possible. Upon my arrival I find very little information on architecture but extensive collections of clothing, tableware, and furnishings from early periods. There is also an extensive display of art and a section devoted to a large collection of weaponry as it has evolved through the years.

I learn that about 450 BC the Boii, who were part of the Celtic peoples, settled in the area and remained until the Docian tribe began to compete with them. It wasn't until the expansion of the Roman Empire that many of the cities of present-day Hungary—Buda, Pest, Pecs, and Györ—began developing into their current form.

Roman influence began to wane around 370 AD when the Huns, a nomadic people from the east, invaded. By 476 AD, the Roman Empire was in serious decline. Following the eventual Roman collapse came the Ostrogoths, the Germanic Lombards, and then the Slavs. In 568 AD, the Slavs were pushed to the south or assimilated by the Avars, another nomadic tribe from the east, but their empire gave way to a new Slavic wave that again dominated the population. By then the populace must have had highly mixed bloodlines from the repeated invasions of diverse ethnic peoples. The seven tribes of the Magyars, coming out of the Ukraine, started their raids on the territory in the 860s and became the nucleus of the kingdom of Hungary. Christianity was not firmly established yet, even though it had first been introduced in Roman times.

The Hungarian Empire expanded until the Turkish conquest and the establishment of the Ottoman Empire in the mid-1500s. In the late 1600s, Austria and its Christian allies regained the territories of the empire from the Ottomans, creating the Great Austro-Hungarian Empire that ruled until 1918. I leave the museum wondering how Hungarian architecture will reflect this past of assorted cultures.

The next morning I drive to the airport to pick up a friend who will be joining me for the remainder of the journey. Elizabeth and I immediately leave for Eger, located in a hilly region on the south slope of the Bükk Mountains. The region has many caves, which have been the home of people since prehistoric times.

We arrive in Eger at dusk, just as the purple sunset is fading. We find a hotel below the fortress and during the evening read about Eger's history. Eger was established as a bishopric by the first king Stephen I of Hungary, in the late 900s or early 1000s, making the town one of Hungary's important cathedral centers. It was overrun in 1241 by the Mongols, who held Eger for the next year. The town reached its peak of medieval development in the late 1300s and 1400s. It returned to its periodic turbulence when the Turks invaded in 1596, occupying the territory for the succeeding ninety-one years. By the mid-1800s, after the purging of the Ottoman Empire, the town had grown to nearly eighteen thousand people.

In the morning we discover that we are on an extension of the Dobo Istvan Square, separated from the rest by a small river. It is market day, and we walk past the vendors who are selling their food and wares, just as they have for centuries.

The Minorita Church, by far the largest building, is in full Baroque glory with its two steeples symbolically reaching skyward to God. The town hall is the next most prominent building on the square. The presence and relative size of the buildings symbolize a powerful alliance between the Church, and what it stood for, and the government. The government building stands as a symbol of authority, organization, protection, and justice. Depending on the government's level of benevolence and competence, in the past people have found a sense of comfort and identity or a feeling of repression. Here I sense a strong alliance between government and Church, and can only guess at how their balance of power has affected people through the years. The rest of the square is surrounded primarily by buildings that house merchants below and living space above.

DOBO ISTVAN SQUARE WITH EGAR BASILICA IN BACKGROUND

Crossing over the river to our hotel, adjacent to a grouping of attractive houses, we have a better view of the Eger Fortress, referred to locally as "the castle." Leading away from the west end of the

MINORITA CHURCH AND TOWN HALL

square are two merchant streets, again with buildings housing shop-keepers below and residents above. To the west, one street leads to the basilica, the only classical building in Eger and the second-largest church in Hungary. Rising above all is the Minaret, the northern-most historical structure from the Turkish era remaining in Europe.

BASILICA OF EGER

We walk along another mixed commercial and residential street,
seeing more architecture with variations that have a pleasing harmony and simple elegance. The ornamentation is prominent but not

MERCHANT STREET

flamboyant or overstated. It is difficult to tell how closely this represents what was here 150 years ago, but we find this impressive
level of refinement throughout Eger.

Back at Dobo Istvan Square, we pass a sculpture of the defending army's battle with the Turks. Elizabeth suggests that the piece expresses power and passion and is an important part of the town's architecture. I realize I have not been paying much attention to statuary so far, and her insight helps me appreciate the symbolic power of sculpture, murals, and fountains and the influences they have on the mood of a space and the emotions that people experience there.

WAR WITH THE TURKS

I wonder how many people who are responsible for placing public artwork today understand the impact of their choices.

After two nights in Eger, we get an early start and head west through the hills toward the Czech Republic. Just out of town Elizabeth points out a unique house with a portico on one side. She recalls seeing several like it along the road approaching Eger.

Before long we spot several more of them and stop to photograph them. Some have special indentations on the side facing the road to hold religious icons and some are embellished with Baroque-style painting. The columned porches generally face in a southern direction, presumably for the advantage of creating a warm area in winter months. On this side of the house there is a fenced yard for gardens, small animals, and a well. As we continue on our way, I wonder how

COTTAGE

the design of these cottages evolved—perhaps a local invention or possibly influences from farther east. In any case, it is another ex-

COTTAGE WITH WELL

ample of architecture that takes advantage of the sun's energy for comfort, much like the solaria used on some of the buildings we saw in Spain.

CESKY KRUMLOV

Cesky Krumlov

The trip to Cesky Krumlov requires a full day of driving through northern Hungary into the Czech Republic. The town lies at the bottom of a small valley carved by the Vltava River, which almost completely encircles the town before winding its way through southern Bohemia to the Moravian Plain.

Looking over my notes along the way, I notice that archaeological discoveries date permanent settlements in the vicinity back to the old stone age, possibly camps of the Neanderthals. There were also mass bronze age settlements by 1500 BC. I am reminded again just how long humans have continually inhabited the same place. Humans moved into each region as the glaciers of the Ice Age retreated, and they adjusted to the gradually changing climate, until now.

The Celtic Boii tribe moved into the area a century before Christ, and the region became known as Bohemia, the Latinized version of their name. Somewhat later the Germanic Morcomari tribe dominated the area, and then the Roman Empire attempted to push north into Bohemia and neighboring Moravia, now part of the Czech lands, but failed to gain a foothold.

In the 500s AD, Slavic tribes inundated the area, displacing and absorbing the Germanic people. The nomadic Huns overtook Hungary and the edges of Moravia in the 800s and 900s but failed to change the composition of Bohemia. Construction of the town and the castle of Krumlov began here in the late 1200s because of the ford in the Vltava River, which for centuries was located on an important trade route. The town took on special importance when it became the residence of the most important nobility in the southern Czech lands, the Rožmberks, who built the extravagant castle on the other side of the river for their home and entertainment.

Although the Turks invaded the lands to the south in the 1500s and were able to dominate Hungary for several hundred years, they did not reach Bohemia. The Hapsburgs of Austria bought the region in 1602, but the dominant Slavic culture, with a minority of Germans and Jews, remained stable as a separate kingdom within the Bavarian and Holy Roman Empires. In the mid-1800s the Bohemian lands were part of the Austrian Empire, but today, after more than a century of turmoil, they form the sovereign nation of the Czech Republic.

Cesky Krumlov, a town of about five thousand people in 1850, served as the center for numerous small villages in the surrounding area, with the district government, district court, and economic and financial centers of the area located here. The region's export economy was based on forestry and glass.

Most of the architecture of the old town and castle was built between the 1300s and the 1600s. In the center of town is Svornosti Square, which is surrounded by the town hall and merchants' homes of Baroque style. A second very narrow square—actually a widened street—is surrounded with more Baroque houses and serves as the marketplace.

BAROQUE HOUSING

Most of the Baroque houses were originally built in a simple Gothic style, usually with vaulted ceilings on the ground floor. In many cases the vaults extend beyond the outer walls, allowing the second level to protrude over the street. In some cases, particularly on Svornosti Square, the houses have arched porticoes to provide covered walks for the merchants' shops below. In the 1500s many of the facades of the houses were redone in highly decorated Renaissance or Baroque styles. Facades on these houses extend up above the pitched roofs, hiding the tile roof coverings. Each house creates

FACADE SGRAFFITO

a unique silhouette where its edge touches the sky. The houses here share a commonality with houses in Eger and Radovljica and with those in the centers of Hallstatt and Kastelruth, with only subtle differences in their embellishments. Today a few houses are being restored to a simpler style, often covering the artfully etched graffito that gives the plastered walls a texture on which figures, scenes, and decorative patterns are painted.

STREET PAST CHAPLIN'S HOUSE

We leave the square and start walking up a narrow street past a house built for the clergy of the adjacent St. Vitus church. Elizabeth notices a five-petal rose carved in stone below a window, which she has heard was used to symbolize Mary Magdalene or the Virgin

CHAPLAIN'S HOUSE

Mary, or to ward off the plague with magical powers. I share with her that, in this region, it represents instead the lineage of rulers from the house of Rozmberk. She counters that both could be true; the families may have gotten the symbol from ancient sources. Its prominence on the chaplain's residence, part of the church, leaves the deeper meaning in question.

TOWER OF CASTLE OF KRUMLOV

Walking back to the plaza and down another street, we see in front of us the tower of the Castle of Krumlov, which is highly decorated in a Rococo style. Such an image certainly has the capacity to enliven a town's inhabitants with a sense of power and pride. The castle, with the Vltava River below snaking its way through Krumlov, has been the seat of authority for this region since the mid-

1200s. The castle underwent extensive reconstruction in the 1500s to bring it up to date with the styles of the Renaissance, lending it its present appearance and stature.

Before leaving Krumlov, we read in the hotel a fellow visitor's description of his stay here years before:

> As if hidden in a palm half open, the town, noted for its scenic beauty and rare grandeur, unfolds before us full of glory and charm of the days bygone. It is a place richly endowed with the bounties of nature and treasures of history, each single element invokes the memories of old days, when people were still at leisure enough to dwell upon details, and to invent a range of artistic solutions to meet their everyday needs.

Leaving Cesky Krumlov the next day, I ponder the implications of the visitor's comment, "each single element invokes the memories of old days, when people were still at leisure enough to dwell upon details, and to invent a range of artistic solutions to meet their everyday needs." That we no longer spend time inventing the range of artistic solutions to meet our everyday needs is a sign that as humans we are not leading lives as fulfilling as they could be. The idea that leisure time is necessary to dwell on detail and employ artistry is a product of the Industrial Revolution, when craftsmen and artisans were replaced by people working like machines, mass producing goods under imposed time constraints, or trained to perform their daily operations as cogs in the office machine. Attention to detail and artistic expression was, for most people, taken away from the workplace. Before the Industrial Revolution, it was not leisure that provided time for artistic expression; artistry was a part of every craftsman, artisan, tailor, weaver, or farmer's working minute. Our architecture, clothing, furniture, glassware—all the items we used and saw around us—were art in their own right. This does not mean that there was not a lot of work that required little or no creativity, but because life moved at a slower pace and there were far fewer distractions, artistic and creative expression had a larger share of everyday life. By the evidence observed so far on this journey, it appears that up until recently people's work and artistic expression have been inseparable.

ROTHENBURG

ROTHENBURG

We leave the Czech Republic and drive through Germany, arriving in late afternoon at the walled town of Rothenburg. Our first glimpse is of a patchwork of crops, vines, fruit trees, and forest with ramparts and buildings above. The surrounding agriculture still provides food for the town as it has for centuries. Crossing the Tauber River, we enter the town through a gated tower. As I look back at

TOWN GATE

MUNICIPAL BUILDING AND TOWN CENTER

LOOKING BACK AT SECOND GATE

the second gate we passed through, I can feel the sense of security the people would have had here through the ages.

We stop in the main town square, centrally located in a grid pattern of streets. The most dominant building is the town hall, which combines Gothic and Renaissance styles. Across from it are houses that are different that possess a harmonious character. In the southeast corner, just behind a large well and fountain pool, are two half-timbered buildings, one of which once had a butcher shop at ground level. We inquire about lodging and find that there are several hotels and private houses that board and provide meals for guests.

NARROW STREET

We walk several blocks down narrow streets to the home of a
Jewish family that offers overnight lodging. We are both anxious to

get our luggage to our rooms so that we can explore the town and observe the architecture, which on our way in appeared to be rich in detail and symbols. As we finish climbing the staircase, Elizabeth remarks on the sensory appeal of the house, which provides a level of intimacy and comfort not present in hotels. The room feels as though it has not changed from Ruskin's time.

SECOND-LEVEL ROOM

Reading about the town's history, I discover that at one point in the Middle Ages, Rothenburg was the second-largest settlement in Germany. At that time it had a population of six thousand, as well as a flourishing center of commerce, probably due to the rich bounty of the surrounding farmlands.

The remains of prehistoric settlements and Stone Age implements dating back to at least 10,000 BC have been found in the area. Unearthed remains indicate that Stone Age people lived here in long, narrow houses supported by poles that were set into the earth and then extended upward to support crossbeams and pitched rafters covered with thatch. Sometime around 500 BC the Celts entered the area and began mixing with the Germanic tribes. The Romans never reached this far north, having stopped forty miles to the south.

In 1142 the Catholic King Konrad III of the Holy Roman Empire erected an imperial castle here, and Rothenburg developed alongside it. King Rudolf of Hapsburg pronounced Rothenburg a free imperial city in 1274, and it ultimately had 180 villages in its domain. In 1311 construction started on the St. James Church, which, when finished in 1485, stood as one of the largest churches of the time, a symbol of the city's great wealth.

From 1258 until the Reformation, a Dominican priory was the home for as many as fifteen hundred nuns. The nuns were from a variety of backgrounds, some of whom chose life in the convent less for religious reasons than as a way to escape a life as an unmarried maiden, poverty, or cruel circumstances. The convent attained great wealth by the end of the 1300s, both through dowries of nuns coming from nobility and wines produced from its vast vineyards in the Tauber Valley.

One verse from the town's museum reveals that life in the convent did not always reflect the Church's doctrines: "We can read about weddings, visits of men, and orgies having taken place in the convent and that the nuns were drinking quite a bit of their wine and having frequent parties with men as their guests. The growing reputation became so embarrassing to the town that the mayor himself had to take matters into his own hands and intervene with the Church. It was the great mayor Heinrich Toppler who finally put an end to those concurrencies."

The town allied itself in 1525 with the leaders of the Peasants' War against the established powers, which included the Church hierarchy. In 1544 the Reformation transformed Rothenburg from Catholic to Protestant, which remains the major religion here. In 1802, after five hundred years of independence, Rothenburg reluctantly agreed to be annexed to the Bavarian Kingdom.

Our first walk around Rothenburg reveals a remarkable collection of both all-stone and half-timbered buildings. The master builder's house, built in 1596 in the Renaissance style, is the most interesting of all. Made from quarried stone, it is decorated with fourteen carved statues representing humanity's seven virtues and seven vices. Other symbols are less obvious. Over the entrance we see a coat of arms, a lion's head, and a grotesque of a man with hoofed feet and

MASTER BUILDER'S HOUSE

hands held to his mouth who seems to be yelling at passersby. Even though we do not understand all the symbols, we find the overall composition of the building well-proportioned and very pleasing to look at. Elizabeth speculates that the odd symbol is a warning to

CREST, LION'S HEAD, AND GROTESQUE

beware, and indeed the grotesque has a repulsiveness that makes me feel uneasy. We move on without knowing what the master builder intended or what the stone sculpture symbolized to the people who lived in his time.

The houses in town are three and four stories tall, with an attic under the steep pitch of reddish tile roofs. The attic space is used for storage; a shuttered opening on the street side with a short boom is used for raising and lowering bags of grain and other items to be stored. In times past, residents were required to maintain a year's

HALF-TIMBERED HOUSE WITH BOOM

supply of wheat, other grains, and salt to assure survival in times of war or poor harvests. Around the exterior of Rothenburg, but within the ramparts, are farmhouses with yards and barns for animals. In

RAMPARTS

medieval times the farmers lived within the walls; the only buildings outside them were occasional secluded barns.

On the second night here, Elizabeth persuades me to follow along with the town night watchman for a while. An actor dressed in medieval costume, he tells stories of the town's past: "In medieval times, as people would depart from the walled city out into the

WATCHTOWER

country they had to obey one rule, and that was to reenter the wall of the village by nightfall. People believed that one could encounter a night fairy if not safely back—and that was held to be a not-so-pleasant experience." I note that even back then with such superstition, indicating a lack of basic understanding of reality, the people produced and lived in fascinating and beautiful architecture that represented them and their culture—who they were and their aesthetic priorities. I am reminded for a moment of my own culture, in which there are still many people, even in leadership roles in government, who adhere to the primitive belief system of the Middle Ages and refuse to accept reality illuminated by science. After an hour we thank the night watchman and walk back to our lodging through the dimly lit streets.

Observing the wonderful variations in architecture has raised as many questions as it has answered, and feeling more invigorated than tired, I am starting to regret that my journey is nearing its end.

HALF-TIMBERED HOUSE

We begin our trip back to England, via Paris, the next day.

The trip is scheduled to take several days, and I want to stop in Burgundy for an extra day to see the villages that produce the famous wines. We decide to stay in Beaune, in the heart of Burgundy, where the wood-framed buildings share much in common with the buildings in Rothenburg.

VILLAGE IN BURGUNDY

The next day, as we make our way to Paris, we are able to get a glimpse of the vineyards, several villages, and the attractive timbered houses typical of the region.

CHIPPING CAMPDEN

CHIPPING CAMPDEN

From Paris we travel to Calais and take a ferry to Dover. We then drive on to Chipping Campden. We find several good inns available for lodging, but I'm feeling somewhat disappointed and reluctant

MARKET HALL

to make a decision about where to stay, because it does not appear there is a village green here, something I was specifically looking for. Noticing my disappointment, Elizabeth suggests that we stay here and search the surrounding villages for a typical green the next day. The town does have an attractive main street, and the market hall looks interesting, so we check in to the Horse & Hound Inn.

The next day we head to Blockley, where we have been told we will find a green. It turns out to be small and on a slope, with houses

MARKET HALL INTERIOR

on two sides, a view of the village on the third, and a church at the lower end. Greens vary tremendously from town to town, but most, including this one, have a well. Many greens also have a stock, a wooden device once used to punish petty criminals.

Village greens are thought to have originated from a need to protect livestock. People would build houses together around a large pasture, allowing cattle, horses, and sheep to be brought in from the surrounding fields for the night. As time passed and villages grew, the green was used less for animals and more for gatherings, festivals, perhaps an occasional traveling circus, and sports such as jousting and other competitive combat. More recently, larger greens have come to be used for cricket, rugby, and soccer. We walk down to the

Looking from the Village Green to Blockley

church at the base of the sloping green and look through the grave-yard to see whether we can find any Corbetts. Norman in origin, the first Corbetts arrived in the Cotswolds after the invasion of William the Conqueror in 1066. Not finding any, we look around for a while for my other English family names: Street, Pottenger, and Beach. My

BLOCKLEY PARISH CHURCH

experience walking through the gravestones pulls me back into the past; everything I see feels remarkably familiar. Relating to the many generations of my ancestors makes me more aware of who I am and what my responsibilities are to future generations. My temporary distraction ends as I find no family names, leaving me to search for my ancestors in other places on another day.

In the church we learn that by the 800s, Blockley had already grown into an important religious center. This church was origi-

GRAVE MARKER

nally built in the late 1000s, after Norman rule began. As is the case throughout England, it was Catholic before Henry VIII made himself head of what became the Church of England. The inside of the church provides a pleasant sense of comfort. Elizabeth finds a shelf with volumes of historical records and spends hours poring through them.

She discovers that in the early years of the Church there were both male and female clerics—priests and deaconesses rather than monks and nuns—who were responsible for teaching and spreading the word around the district. Their efforts were directed at some of the local people in the north Cotswolds who were still pagans—Anglos who worshipped the Norse gods Wooton, Thor, and Fricke.

Blockley is not unusual in having its own church; it seems that all villages, large and small, have one. Broad Campden, a village adjacent to Chipping Campden, has remnants of a small Norman chapel that was built in the 1000s and named after St. Mary Magdalene, later to be replaced by a new church across the road.

ROW HOUSES

Late in the afternoon, as we were heading back to Chipping Campden, Elizabeth and I pass individual cottages and row houses

THATCHED ROOF HOUSE

and are fascinated with their scale and composition. We can see and feel a special charm and their happy and inviting character. After

THATCHED ROOF COTTAGE

months of travel and seeing so many different styles of houses in so many different settings—all true reflections of the local people, their

CHIPPING CAMPDEN

culture, and the surroundings—I now see the importance begun to see a house as the symbol of home. Throughout human existence, whether in the mouth of a cave, a hut, or a modern house, home is where humans have experienced comfort and safety. From birth through our early years, we become aware of our home as our protective shell. It is where we can show a considerable degree of personal expression, and through the years it is where we take refuge in privacy with the family. In many ways the home is an extension of the dweller's identity. A symbol of a the family unit, a home also helps fulfill a variety of the emotional needs of each family member. For some reason, the houses I am seeing here, on the road to Chipping Camden, more than any others, convey to me that symbology—a reaction that is no doubt personal and based on my cultural heritage and my past experiences.

As we reach the top of a hill we can see Chipping Campden in a shallow valley of the Cotswolds, a range of low hills in the central part of England. The village appears tranquil and fixed, as though it has existed here from the beginning of time. I know, though, that the permanence I feel is misleading. Like all the other towns and villages I have visited, this place has had layer upon layer of habitation by one culture after another. And, as elsewhere, here once lived people from a prehistoric time, people physically and mentally like us who have left little that might help us understand just how they lived and viewed the world. What archeological evidence there is reveals that humans inhabited this area as early as 10,000 BC with agricultural settlements here dating back to 3000 BC. Historians believe that Campedene, as it was once called, means "fields or enclosures in the valley."

The Celtic culture—the regional tribe being known as the Dobunni—dates back here to about 450 BC. The people—ultimately a mix of those who migrated from mainland Europe and the native people—prospered by farming the rich lime-clay soils with abundant springs. During these early times, hilltop forts gave way to small hamlets of wood-frame houses where tribal groups were the predecessors of small kingdoms.

The Roman invasion of Britain in 43 AD brought a competing culture and superior technologies. It is likely that Roman domination left an intermingled population close to its towns and villas, with a separate Celtic culture from the fringes outward, each influencing the other. The Roman methods of building stone houses or houses built on a stone foundation were passed down because of their durability and longevity. With the fall of the Roman Empire the Saxons invaded the area, bringing their language and culture. At that time timber construction typical of that on the German plain and similar to what we saw near Beaune and in Rothenburg became popular. By the late 600s the Anglo-Saxon settlers, known as Hwicce, had started to coexist in this part of Britain with the Celts. The Celts remained somewhat separate, with continual conflict springing up between the two cultures. The Normans from Normandy invaded in the 1000s, adding one more culture to the mix, but the Celtic influence has remained strong in parts of England, Wales, Scotland, and Ireland to the present day.

With a prospering wool business, Chipping Campden grew as it filled with merchants, traders, and wealthy landowners. A local historian writes, "In about 1185, Campden was granted permission by King Henry II to hold a market and a prefix 'Chipping' from the old English word 'ceping', meaning market, was added. The borough of Campden was developed at this time with a high street, market square, and long burgage plots of the 'burgesses,' mostly craftsmen and traders." When I see this, I immediately remember the burgher houses in Radovljica, Slovenia. I realize now that they were houses for the middle class, the bourgeoisie, and that their styles varied by region. The elongated burgage plots I see fronting High Street offer the resident a house with a storefront and a small farm behind, accessible from the street through an archway. This unique configuration allows space for animals, fruit trees, and gardens.

Chipping Campden differs from most of the towns I have visited so far in that it grew along a road, with houses and merchants' shops spread out from end to end. Campden's main road is broad, allowing for markets and other activities, an alternative to the village green. Architectural styles are mixed, with the oldest Gothic house dating back to 1380. The alms houses that were built in 1612 were of high quality, affording the pensioners who have lived there through the years an unusual bit of luxury.

ALMS HOUSES

The buildings here are made of a honey-colored limestone. Moderately steep roofs are covered with flat stone or thatch and have mostly gable ends with gable and shed-roofed dormers. Most thatched roofs in town have given way to flat stone, although many thatched houses remain along the road and in the surrounding villages.

According to the information from the town's museum, much of the significant public architecture was commissioned by a single individual. In the early 1600s Baptist Hicks, a London merchant and moneylender who was lord of the manor, built the Market Hall, the alms houses near St. James' Church, and opposite them his residence, the old Campden House. Most of it was destroyed in 1645 during the Civil War. After walking along the terrace of the alms houses, we continue toward the lodges and gateway and banqueting

LODGES AND GATEWAY

house of Baptist Hicks, all that remains of the extensive residence that was built in 1610. Not much is left to be seen through the gate, at least not without climbing the stone wall, so we circle around the church and peer through the cemetery at the banqueting house. It has a strange and eerie ambience, perhaps in part because it is set next to a graveyard. I notice that the spirals are similar to those on the top of the church. This gives an air of pretentiousness to the building, or perhaps it is just that their proportion seems awkward.

The next day we leave Chipping Campden wondering about Baptist Hicks and what motivated his philanthropy. How did he obtain his great wealth? What were his political or fraternal associations, and why was his house a target for destruction during the Civil War? We leave even more aware of how the differences in design from place to place were filled with meaning for the builders and people during times when life did not have the complicated

HICK'S BANQUETING HOUSE

distractions of the modern world. This was a time before mass communication and industrial production of goods and services created a standardization of culture across the world.

HAWKSHEAD

Hawkshead

Hawkshead village lies in the Vale of Esthwaite between lakes Windermere and Coniston in northern England. After a day's drive from Chipping Campden, we enter the hills of Cumbria, where a dense forest opens up into hills covered with heather and bracken. From there we travel around the side of Lake Windermere, with its choppy waters fed by fast-flowing brooks tumbling over black mossy rocks.

The area gets limited sunlight, and fertile soil is scarce, making grazing sheep and cows the best use of the land. Apples are the only cultivated fruit, although berries and chestnuts grow in the wild.

We enter a shallow valley where dense forests have been cleared of brush along the stream to provide pasture for cows and sheep, and spot an occasional fleeing rabbit. Among the trees and rock outcroppings, the animals always add to the picturesque scene. As we come over a slight rise, we can see in the distance a dark stone church on a hill just slightly above Hawkshead's white houses with their gray slate roofs. A poem William Wordsworth wrote on his return from Cambridge in 1788 suggests that the church was once white:

> I saw the snow-white church upon the hill
> Sit like a throned lady sending out
> A gracious look all over her domain.

As we get closer, we pass by farmhouses with chimneys of differing shapes extending through the slate roofs. Moss-covered stone walls at their edges enclose sheep and cattle.

FARMHOUSE

We pull into the market square and enter the King's Arms Inn, taking rooms right above the bar. A little later our innkeeper joins us for dinner .With a steady mist falling outside and a blazing fire that warms the body and soul, we sip a pleasant amber ale in front of the fireplace. Then, under the low wood-beam ceiling, we enjoy a supper of lamb stew with bread and butter. The innkeeper tells us that parts of the building may date back as far as six hundred years, when buildings began life as timbered construction with wattle-and-daub walls and roofs of turf, heather, or bracken. The rebuilding in stone began in the 1600s, but many of the oak beams and panels remain from the original building.

In its earliest known history, Hawkshead was a stockaded settlement built by a Norseman leader named Haukr. The Norsemen were from the Irish island, where they had been in contact with Catholic and Celtic traditions. From the 1100s until the dissolution

MARKET SQUARE

of the Catholic Church by Henry VIII, the area was administered by the Cistercians of Furness Abbey, located on the coast to the west. In the 1200s, monks from the abbey built a manor house here for their residence.

The parish church of St. Michael and All Angels, on a hill above the village, where a pagan temple once stood, began as a chapel dating back to the 1100s and took its final form in about 1500. The church's interior of dark wood and white plaster has carefully articulated detail. The dark ceiling trusses and dark pews contrast with the white walls and arches, leaving me with a feeling much like that experienced in the Basque church in Sare. These light, airy churches leave me in the present, a place where interaction among people seems easy. The other churches, by contrast, were darker inside, more massive in construction and, like the cave at Altamira, imposing and powerful. In them I experienced the feeling of being outside of time, or being in the presence of some indescribable power, a place where

ST. MICHAEL AND ALL THE ANGELS CHURCH

the dominance of the architecture takes away any desire to talk or relate to other people around you.

As we leave this church with its warm and friendly atmosphere and walk through the cemetery, the Celtic influence is apparent. The cemetery contains many grave markers with Celtic ornamentation— very different from the markers in Chipping Campden, where sym- bols of the French Normans were dominant.

GRAMMAR SCHOOL

In 1585 the Archbishop of York, Edwin Sandys, a native of the parish, founded and endowed the town's grammar school. From the school's inception, admission was granted only to boys from the families of nobles—priests and bishops, judges, lawyers, wealthy merchants, and farmers with considerable landholdings. An entrance test was required, and school went year-round without intermission except for three weeks at Christmas and again at Easter. The school day was from 6:00 a.m. to 5:00 p.m. Monday through Friday, and from 6:00 a.m. to 2:00 p.m. on Saturday. Church was mandatory on Sunday.

Hawkshead's main road winds through the town, passing close to the school and market square. The wealthy live in manor houses outside the town, and small hamlets with farms and cottages are

NARROW STREET

scattered throughout the surrounding countryside. Inside the town are cottages, merchant houses, and six inns. On the square is a market building that had butcher's stalls at ground level and merchants on the floor above. The inn where we are staying lies opposite the market building, with merchant houses on the other two sides. Four streets lead into the square, one through a covered passageway from

STREET TO MARKET SQUARE

the east. A separate pathway goes from the square up the hill to the church, which is directly behind the market building. The scale of the houses and buildings, some with bare stone but most with plaster and whitewash, is smaller here in Hawkshead than in all the

REMAINS OF GLASTONBURY ABBEY

previous towns and villages and produces a surprisingly comfortable feeling. The organic street layout creates a more relaxed feeling than the planned towns with a grid pattern.

Wordsworth, who was on a quest to keep rail lines out of the region, was schooled here and wrote many poems inspired by the natural beauty of the surroundings. The area has been frequented by other poets, artists, and writers, including John Ruskin, whose attention to the pristine atmosphere in the Lake District speaks to how special this region is. The home in which he lived for the latter part of his life, his "villa," as he referred to it, is nearby on Lake Coniston. Beatrix Potter also lived on a farm a few miles away, using the quaintness of the architecture and natural scenery as an inspiration for her storybooks.

Even though I am enjoying the beauty of the countryside and the houses, I am eager to visit Glastonbury and Stonehenge, so we leave early and after a day's drive arrive in Glastonbury for a planned two-night stay. This leaves time for a short stop at Stonehenge, an absolute priority for me, before sailing home to the United States from Southampton.

During our first morning in Glastonbury, we

FIVE PETAL ROSE

explore the remains of the famous abbey, which was destroyed by King Henry VIII in retribution for disobedience by the local clergy. Elizabeth excitedly points out a remnant from the abbey or possibly one of the accompanying buildings—a depiction of the five-petal rose with a crown on top and animals on each side. She wonders aloud whether it could represent King Arthur, Guinevere, or Mary Magdalene, who in myth are all associated with the area or another royal family. A man stops us, bringing us out of our reverie.

"Have you heard?" he asks. "The roadways around London have been closed. All airports in the country have been shut down. A terrorist threat is in progress. People are being asked to stay where they are and not to try to travel."

The disturbing news shocks us right back into the realities of the present global situation. We pack quickly, pay our bill, and depart from our bed-and-breakfast, wanting to be absolutely sure we get to Southampton before our ship sails. But I cannot resist the temptation to make a brief stop at Stonehenge. As I walk around the roped-off stones I am struck immediately by their massiveness and marvel at the effort needed to transport them from miles away. What was it that so powerfully motivated the builders of this and other dolmens some forty-five hundred years ago? They must surely have intended to build a lasting and permanent creation, but to what end? Was it a site for healing or other spiritual rituals or what they believed to be a home for the souls of their ancestors? Was it to record an extraordinary event or idea that changed their perception of the world? While we do know that the stones are arranged in accordance with the sun's movement, the site engenders the feeling that there must be a deeper meaning, something that they knew or believed that we do not yet understand.

After our brief visit to Stonehenge, we drive toward Southampton without hearing any new information about the terrorist threat. Although our extra day in Southampton turns out to have been unnecessary, our precaution has served to ease our worries. There are signs of heightened security as we board our ship, among them dogs sniffing luggage, yet a calm and courteous atmosphere prevails.

Our arrival in New York six days later proves quite a different story. After disembarking from our ship, before we even reach the customs inspection station, we walk through a long, narrow room past fifteen or so soldiers from different armed forces, all holding automatic weapons and looking out with sober, unfriendly faces.

Although this abrupt ending to my journey jolts me back into twenty-first-century reality, somehow, after my return, I feel different. As Elizabeth and I head back to California by train, I feel like a time traveler from the Middle Ages, out of place in today's world; a person moved emotionally by the magical power from each place I visited. I feel as though a spell has been cast by the artists centuries ago on all who would later view their work. It is clear that the depth of feelings and emotions I experienced come from the genuineness and richness of detail of the artists' expression.

Now, after this journey, I feel an additional weight as I compare today's relatively flimsy architecture, lacking in artistry, with what building and architecture were like when the medieval master builders were designing and building houses, churches, and cathedrals. Having seen how human life has existed for thousands of years, linked by chains of succeeding cultures, each maintaining a balance with nature, I can't help but fear that ours could be the last link in the chain if we don't awaken and optimize our human sensibilities and make crucial adjustments to the way we live and build. The permanence of the communities I saw from the past and the growing instability of what we have today compel me to believe that the next twenty years will be a crucial juncture in time where only quick and effective action will allow us some control over our destiny.

As the train rolls on mile after mile, I contemplate everything I have seen and felt on my journey through times past and what has happened since. I think back to my building of Village Homes in Davis, California, in the 1970s. It was an attempt to create a distinct sense of place, to use the sun's energy to heat the homes, to incorporate food production into the neighborhoods, and to create places and space for community activities and festivities. It was designed to respect the processes of nature and encourage the individuality of the people who live there. When I compare it to the unsightly tract developments that have sprung up throughout the world in the last forty years, as small independent home builders have been replaced by large corporate contractors who care little for the environment, or even their customers' needs, I feel discouraged. But my journey has left me optimistic because if there was once consistent beauty in our surroundings, if there was once a poetry of architecture, then we can restore that element of civilization as we take on the challenges of a new era. We can redesign and rebuild our communities with grace and beauty, and in such a way that the life-support systems of our planet are integrated, nurtured and sustained so that they can in turn nurture and sustain us.

CHAPTER IV

THE RETURN OF THE CITY-STATE

*To Counter Corporate Power and
Regain Local Political, Economic, and Architectural Control*

I started my own design and construction business in 1967, after an apprenticeship with the architectural firm of John Carl Warneke and Associates in San Francisco, California, and took the title of master builder to indicate that I was combining the practice of designing and building the way it was during medieval times. In 1973 I found investors and 70 acres of undeveloped land in Davis, California and began a project that would allow me to put my ideas about aesthetics, solar energy production and environmentally sensitive design into practice. My success in building Village Homes rested on my ability to convince financial institutions and the city of Davis that the project's new environmental concepts were viable.

When I first presented the design for Village Homes to the planning department, the head official told me, "The design flies in the face of everything I learned in college." Her response was no surprise. The development incorporated environmentally friendly innovations that broke a number of regulations for residential development. I was instantly at loggerheads with convention in a world I knew would have to change. Fortunately, the Davis City Council was progressive, and approved the project over the objections of the planning, public Works, fire, and police departments. This was a bold action, one of many taken by the city of Davis during an era in which its municipal practices were being reconsidered. In fact, Davis, along with a few other jurisdictions in the country, sparked a movement towards solar energy, energy efficiency, recycling and growth management, one that inspired change around the world. The council at that time embodied Descartes' notion, noted in chapter 2, that people should "never. . . accept anything for true which [they] did not clearly know to be such." It refused to take the easy, conservative approach recommended by its staff, and instead took the time to gain a deeper understanding of the issues. Like the city-states of old, Davis established local standards that anticipated the needs of its citizens.

Completed in 1982, Village Homes quickly became world renowned for its innovation, and since its inception has been continually visited by dignitaries, architects, planners and activists from around the world. Unfortunately, in the ensuing thirty years residential design has moved in the opposite direction, with the proliferation of sprawling, unsightly and environmentally unfriendly development throughout the United States and other countries. The enlightened decision-makers, it turned out, were rare. Most jurisdictions accepted the visions of large-scale residential developers, leaving their towns and cities far less attractive than they once were, lacking in festive spaces for community activities and highly dependent on the automobile.

The time has come to try again. Our economy is struggling, the overstimulation and chaos in today's world is straining the mental health of the population and the life-support systems of our planet are starting to collapse. If we are to survive, we must rapidly adopt a truly civilized lifestyle. We must transform our architecture—our homes and buildings, our transportation systems, our industries and our agriculture—so that it nurtures our spirits and heals the wounds we have inflicted on the environment. The impetus for change will not come from the urge to make our living environment more beautiful; too many people are unaware of what is missing and of the importance of our visual world to our health and well-being. It will instead come from the continuing collapse of our environment, which will stir us to act by awakening our instinct for survival.

As the consequences of climate change become more widely recognized, people will want to know how they will be affected, how they can help solve the problem, and ultimately, as conditions worsen, where they can find the most comfortable and safest places to live. Those of us who are already deeply concerned are looking for political leadership to slow earth's rapid climate change and minimize its impacts. But politics will follow the people, and it is we the people who must work for change now.

Given the complexity of national and global politics and the power of corporations, the quickest route to change is at the local level. Looking back through time, we see that city-states, free towns, and local jurisdictions historically provided the highest degree of citizen participation in governance. Local governments set standards for public behavior, offered protection, provided infrastructure, determined land use issues and provided many other social functions. City-states and free towns rivaled kingdoms and empires for the allegiance of their people, with the local power more often than not commanding the most loyalty. In *On the Medieval Origins of the Modern State*, published in 1970, Joseph R. Strayer writes:

> In the ancient world, states tended to fall into two classes: the great, imperfectly integrated empires, and the small, but highly cohesive units such as the Greek city-states. Each type had weaknesses. The empires were militarily strong, but could enlist only a small proportion of their inhabitants in the political process or, indeed, in any activity that transcended immediate local interests. . . .The city-state made far more effective use of its inhabitants than the empire; all citizens participated actively in the political process and in associated community activities.[1]

City-states and similarly independent towns often controlled the surrounding land and villages as well. On some occasions city-states became powerful, expanding and becoming kingdoms or even empires. This is how the Roman Empire came to be. But as a rule, more often they retained a smaller scale more conducive to true democratic participation. The Greek and Roman city-states and the free towns of the Middle Ages were the places where individuals found the most freedom of mind and in which the arts, science, philosophy and civil society made the most progress. City-states and free towns had an easily understandable social structure and an orderly and aesthetically pleasing architecture that fit well within their surroundings. Aristotle, whose writing on ethics heavily influenced the religions of the Western world and who was the dominant influence on Western thinking until the ascendancy of Descartes, proclaimed that city-states should function for the sole purpose of ensuring a good life for their people. He regarded the "political partnership" between city-state and citizens as existing in order to foster noble action rather than being simply a living arrangement.[2] It is still true that local jurisdictions potentially have the greatest influence on our quality of life and exist—or should exist—to ensure that noble action is taken to provide for a high quality of life.

As the Middle Ages drew to a close, the power of towns and cities was weakened as national governments reined in their autonomy. By the beginning of the twentieth century, national governments, both democratic and autocratic, were the most powerful entities in the world and relinquished only what power they chose to state and local governments and corporate interests. Gradually, however, as corporations continued to grow into global empires, power shifted yet again until by the end of the twentieth century corporations had gained control in one way or another over much of the earth's resources, means of production, communications, finances, transportation, medicine and food supplies. These corporations heavily influence politicians through contributions and the citizenry through their products and advertising.

The power wielded by what I call the Empire of Global Corporations rests largely on our addiction to the lifestyle they advocate and our dependence on what they produce. As one who shares that addiction, I understand how people have succumbed. We assimilate corporate propaganda into our worldview, unaware of the control it exerts on us. For some, loyalty to the corporate network stems from the jobs and livelihood it provides; for most, it comes from Madison Avenue advertisers who have ensured that conspicuous consumerism is imprinted daily, if not hourly, onto our collective psyche. The lifestyle that this empire zealously promotes rivals the doctrines of religion and the very fundamentals of democracy for the hearts and minds of the people. Taken as a whole, The Empire may be more powerful than all other entities, whether governmental, religious, or private.

It would be foolish to wait for The Empire to take the lead in addressing the problems of global warming. Decisions at the corporate level are made based on profit motives and a short-term perspective. In addition, as a result of the economic meltdown of 2008–2009, we know that corporations are not dependable mainstays of society. We have seen the heads of corporations arrogantly drive their institutions to bankruptcy, wreaking havoc on investors, the public, the environment and the economy, while they walked away from the crash with their personal fortunes enhanced. However, the corporations will ultimately respond to the will of their customers, a dynamic that makes obvious the need for grassroots community education and activism, with people selecting only those products and services that are environmentally and socially responsible and patronizing only those businesses that share a similar ethos.

While some prominent national and state government leaders are now addressing global warming, a promising sign, action will likely be slow here as well, in part because of corporate influence on legislation. Nevertheless, we must encourage our representatives to push for needed change. For instance, we need a direct carbon tax on all fossil fuels, imported or domestic. Without such a tax, we are consuming carbon energy without paying for its long-term impacts, costs that economists call "externalities." Future generations are already going to have to pay for the last hundred years of fossil fuel use as they contend with the earth's collapsing life-support systems. The revenues of this carbon tax could offset some of the impact of fossil fuels on global warming and their cumulative damage to the environment by building an efficient rail transportation system, reforesting, and developing alternative power sources. Denis Hayes, former director of the Solar Energy Research Institute under the Carter administration, advocates the implementation of a direct carbon tax. In his article, *A Plan for the Solar Revolution*, he writes:

> If we could adopt a system that economists call an "upstream cap and 100-percent auction," such a system would eventually produce hundreds of billions of dollars a year. At the same time, it would steer energy investments away from carbon-intensive fuels such as oil, coal, liquids from coal, bituminous sands and oil shale. This is the climate strategy most likely to alter the world's energy markets before irreversible harm is done.[3]

The power to implement such a plan rests in the hands of the U.S. Congress and President, but it is the people who must create the political will, at the same time that we make changes in our own lifestyles and local jurisdictions to accommodate a fossil-fuel-free future. Our struggle to overcome our reliance on fossil fuels as quickly as needed is complex: our social, architectural and economic infrastructures have tied us inextricably to them. Even if we could stop using fossil fuels tomorrow, a sudden curtailment in their use would in the short term create more instant and widely felt hardship than that caused by the increasing yet subtler effects of climate change. But when projected over a decade or two, those subtle and gradual effects lead to a series of devastating consequences, making it imperative that we take action sooner rather than later.

The prevalent strategy for solving the problem of global warming has been to focus on more efficient ways of using fossil fuels (e.g., more efficient appliances, furnaces and automobiles). Such efforts are necessary, but in isolation, they merely delay the inevitable. Over the next ten to twenty years we will have to drastically reduce the use of fossil fuels, both because they are a finite resource that will become increasingly expensive and, more importantly, because they are destroying our hospitable environment. The timetable for reducing greenhouse gases by 80 percent by the year 2050 is a political compromise that has been bandied about, but it is simply not serious enough. It represents too much of a gamble, as we could well pass the point of no return for maintaining a livable planet. An 80 percent reduction by the year 2020 is a goal that increases the potential for human survival. Lester R. Brown, in his book *Plan B 3.0: Mobilizing to Save Civilization*, spells out a comprehensive plan to accomplish this goal. His plan goes beyond the need to cut greenhouse gasses and focuses attention on the shift to local economies that will result from the shift to renewable sources. Brown emphasizes that our primary goal has to be to cut carbon emissions but that secondary goals must include stabilizing the population, eradicating poverty and restoring the earth's ecosystems. He writes:

> Whereas fossil fuels helped globalize the energy economy, shifting to renewable sources will localize it. We anticipate that the energy transition will be driven largely by mounting concerns about climate change, by climbing oil prices, and by the restructuring of taxes to incorporate the

indirect costs of burning fossil fuels. It is encouraging to know that we now have the technologies to build a new energy economy, one that is not climate-disruptive, that does not pollute the air, and that can last as long as the sun itself. The question is no longer whether we can develop a climate-stabilizing energy economy, but whether we can develop it before climate change spins out of control.[4]

What is needed, then, is a speedy but orderly transition to alternative fuels and power sources—solar, geothermal, wind, and biomass. Building a new alternative energy economy will be difficult because of the influence wielded by the oil industry, whose megacorporations sit atop the Empire of Global Corporations and whose leaders will not easily give up the power and profits they derive from the value of their oil, gas, and coal resources and production capacity. But regardless of their influence, change will undeniably occur, whether out of political mandate or economic or environmental necessity.

What are the environmental and economic events that will hasten this shift? Although global warming will affect everyone in various ways, the most drastic changes will be to the poor and to those living in areas most subject to drought, heat waves, wildfires, water shortages, rising sea levels and severe storms. Prices for energy, water, and food will at some point escalate as a result of the inevitable shortage in fossil fuels or of a carbon tax. Inflationary pressure from these increases will drive up prices for most other goods. As the population moves from climatically or economically threatened areas, homes will decrease in value or be left vacant. Later, as global warming continues to have increasingly severe effects, large cities that have high energy demands and reduced water supplies and little or no availability of locally produced food will become increasingly expensive and uncomfortable. If we do nothing to change those places, they could become desolate.

Other areas will likely feel the pressures of population growth. People will be attracted to places where there is an adequate water supply, where there are moderate temperatures that make the heavy use of air conditioning unnecessary, where there is still a local agricultural economy that provides a steady supply of healthy food, where residents are not required to drive long distances and can conveniently get to where they want to go on foot, bicycle, or by public transit, and where they are able to find satisfying entertainment within their own community. In these places, healthy economies will provide the resources for good law enforcement to keep crime rates low—an additional attraction. With the material and economic resources that such places have will come the political desire to control those resources and to ensure their availability. People from other areas will surely seek out such locations. Housing prices will rise. Some families might have to share larger homes for economic benefit, much as we have seen at other times in history, such as during the phylloxera epidemic that killed the wine industry in Arcos de la Frontera (discussed in chapter 3). When most people lived in small towns and villages, as in the mid-1800s, humanity's footprint was lighter on the earth. These towns and villages are the kinds of places that will fare the best because of their ability to be easily transformed back into self-sustaining communities.

If the predictions presented here seem strange or unlikely, just look back through history, as we have done in the preceding chapters, and you can see how changing political and environmental conditions have caused people to move, settlements to either swell or be abandoned and civilizations to reform or collapse. The ordinary course of human history shows us that people have always had to adapt by changing where and how they lived or else perish in their refusal to do so.

The transition to an alternative fuel economy will have a dramatic effect on transportation, the value of human labor and the nature of our economy, as energy from renewable sources is more expensive to produce and provides for a much lower net energy return. Instead of receiving eighteen to thirty units of energy for every unit of energy used in its production, as is the case with cheap fossil fuels, we will receive only two to ten units of energy for every one unit used in the production of alternatives. To make up the difference, we must devise new strategies that maximize efficiency, reduce transportation miles, expand local economies and change industrial production methods. These changes will be painful only if we insist on continuing our current consumption-based lifestyles and do not redesign and retrofit our architecture. If we look to pre-Industrial towns and villages for inspiration, however, we can see this as an opportunity to bring back many of the aesthetic and lifestyle qualities we have lost.

As we move forward, there will be ongoing power struggles among national, state, and local governments, with cities and towns seeking to retain local tax money and the autonomy to enact policies and set standards locally. Local regulations that address regional environmental problems are typically at odds with both corporate interests and government standards, which the corporations often help write. Arguing that it would be difficult to produce different designs for individual communities or regions, corporations seek federal or state help in striking down such laws or in preempting them with much more lenient state or federal regulations. Federal regulations have also helped to create a more sterile, standardized world, with laws that, even when otherwise intended, end up supporting corporate business. As a result, smaller businesses, which respond better to local needs, have been driven out of the market, leaving us with products that only marginally address regional differences while concentrating economic power in entities that are centralized rather than local. Retaining power on the local level is crucial to creating real change, but winning these battles for our communities will require continual vigilance and relentless pressure on our elected officials.

Within this context, how can we redesign and rebuild our cities, towns and neighborhoods today in a way that reduces our use of fossil fuels and ensures our survival? We can start by minimizing the need for vehicular transportation—one of the biggest users of fossil fuels. This will require the transformation of our existing urban and suburban sprawl into a system of walkable villages, much like the self-contained towns of old, in which jobs, stores, professional offices, entertainment and education are all available locally. This change in our public spaces and modes of transportation will also encourage the healthy social interactions that have enriched human life through the centuries.

Movements to implement more efficient and human-scale development—alternatives to the auto-oriented growth that has reigned over the last hundred years—have occurred periodically from the early part of the twentieth century to the present New Urbanist movement. For most of the last century, these alternative efforts have been aimed at mitigating the impact of cars and trucks by creating off-street pedestrian routes. In 1937, under the direction of Guy Tugwell's Federal Resettlement Administration, Rex Ford designed and built Greenbelt, Maryland, the first of three "green towns" that were part of President Franklin Roosevelt's New Deal. Promoted by First Lady Eleanor Roosevelt and modeled after the English garden cities planned in the late nineteenth century, the purpose of these "green" projects was to provide employment and affordable housing in pleasant, healthy surroundings for low-income families during the Great Depression. Greenbelt took its name from the belt of green forest-land around it and from the swaths of green between neighborhoods that allowed the architecture and people to remain in close contact with nature. The town was composed of masonry townhouses, prefabricated detached houses and garden apartments. It was laid out with superblocks and a system of interior walkways that permitted residents to go from home to town center separated from vehicle traffic and without major street crossings. Shops, schools, ball fields and community buildings were located in the center of the town. Greenbelt has continued through the years to provide its inhabitants with the benefits of natural beauty and reduced exposure to the automobile, but the commercial center lost its vigor when sprawling subdivisions and shopping malls grew around the town's periphery.

Although this type of development remained rare, it inspired others throughout the century. One of the most prominent was Reston, Virginia, a master-planned city composed of seven villages—walkable communities that were integrated with their original rural surroundings—each with its own shopping and community center. The village of Lake Ann, for example, has an attractive center built with contemporary architecture on a traditional piazza, a place with vibrant social interaction. The village was designed around an artificial lake, and its center is completely separated from roads, with parking at one end and pedestrian walkways that penetrate the surrounding neighborhoods. Stores, offices and restaurants face the piazza at ground level, with apartments and offices above.

Reston's overall design, a system of villages, included thirty-five churches, fifteen elementary schools, three intermediary schools, three high schools, and one community college, as well as a regional center with a medical complex, transportation terminal, hotel, conference center and multipurpose auditorium. A full range of recreation facilities—a swimming pool, tennis courts and golf course—was included as well. The natural areas in and around the villages provided a beautiful setting for the homes and community centers, and the architecture was built to a high standard that has since become increasingly rare as large corporate builders began to dominate the industry.

Despite its best intentions, the project had its limitations. Its lack of mass transit and its location (outside the Washington, DC metropolitan area) meant that, although the project was not visually dominated by the automobile, inhabitants were nevertheless highly dependent on their cars. And while Reston itself fulfilled its own ideals, its influence has, like Greenbelt's, been overpowered by the massive development and urban sprawl that has occurred beyond its perimeter.

In the early 1970s, I started the plans for Village Homes, attempting to create a new model for environmentally sensitive, community-oriented development. My vision, much like Rex Ford's and inspired by the ideas of Louis Mumford, Clarence Stein and the Regional Planning Association of America, was to de-emphasize the automobile by separating cars from pedestrians. As in Greenbelt, I used paths and greenways throughout the seventy-acre community to connect the houses to the village center, and eliminated through automobile traffic. But car use is just one of the many environmental issues associated with development; I wanted to do more. I came up with three other significant innovations that set Village Homes apart.

The first was the use of solar energy. With an average of nearly two hundred sunny days per year, Davis is ideally situated to harness the sun's energy. The houses in Village Homes are oriented for passive solar heating and natural cooling; each has a domestic solar water heating system, and some have active solar heating as well. As a result, houses requires about 50 percent less energy on average than homes that were built at the same time with conventional heating and cooling systems.

The second innovation was the integration of edible landscaping within the community. It seemed as though there was no reason that the land and resources that traditionally went into ornamental landscaping could not be used for food production. Most noticeable are the orchards, vineyards and large vegetable plots around the periphery and along the greenways. There are also individual fruit and nut trees used as ornamental plantings. To assure the highest productivity from the land, we planted vines and fruit trees around the houses, with vegetable gardens in the yards and in the adjacent commons. Having an extensive local source of tasty vine-ripened food saves energy that otherwise goes to the transportation and refrigeration of food brought to local grocery stores. Having lived in Village Homes for twenty years, I know firsthand that families can produce at least half of the fresh fruits and vegetables they consume.

Finally, the design incorporated surface rainwater drainage swales, a system that allows rainwater to penetrate the earth, where it accumulates and is stored for use by trees and shrubs during dry weather, thereby reducing the amount of water needed for year-round irrigation. Standard procedure, in contrast, is to collect rainwater from roofs, driveways and yards and then funnel it into street gutters and from there to underground storm drains, a system that carries away as much as 90 percent of the water, causing rapid run-off and erosion problems downstream from the development. In Village Homes, most rainwater is retained onsite and the small amount that does run off is cleaned as it trickles through the grassy swales. In addition to its environmental benefits and cost savings, natural drainage adds considerably to the landscape architect's ability to delight the senses with the interwoven texture of streams, ponds, stonework and plants that make visible the natural process of rain falling to the earth and being collected. The sound of running water as it spills over rocks and small wood dams enhances the experience.

Village Homes quickly became a popular place to live, as much for the rural feeling and picturesque setting created by the orchards, vineyards, gardens and natural waterways as for its innovative solar energy features. But as with other islands of innovation, while it provides an instructive model for solar energy use, edible landscaping and natural drainage, it still leaves its residents highly dependent on the automobile. Although there is a small village center containing offices, a restaurant, a dance studio, a pool and a community building, only a few of its residents can actually work in Village Homes and the goods and services available there are limited.

Taking inspiration from developments like these, the New Urbanists of the 1980s and '90s renewed efforts to create walkable, self-contained communities on a human, rather than automobile, scale. Using the classical grid street pattern and de-emphasizing the automobile in other ways, builders of these communities have produced outstanding examples of new and redevelopment projects. One of the first was Seaside, located in the Florida panhandle on the shores of the Gulf of Mexico. Created in 1981 by architects Andrés Duany and Elizabeth Plater-Zyberk and developer Robert Davis, Seaside is built on a "village" scale and is designed to foster a sense of community. Walkways crisscross the development to encourage walking and biking, while narrow streets serve to reduce traffic speed. Building fronts are a uniform distance from the curb, and all the streets are tree-lined. The community center creates a gathering place, with stores, schools and the post office all located within a five-minute walk of each dwelling. Even though the village has ended up with a high percentage of vacation homes, the eighty-acre project exemplifies most of the principles of the New Urbanist movement: "The built environment must be diverse in use and population. . . scaled for the pedestrian yet capable of accommodating the automobile and mass transit. . . and. . .have a well defined public realm supported by an architecture that reflects the ecology and culture of the region." The architects' attention to design and detail at Seaside truly expresses the poetry of architecture.

Other recent projects from the New Urbanists model for us the possibility of transforming our existing urban architecture into aesthetically pleasing, environmentally sensitive villages through careful redevelopment. One such project, situated near downtown Atlanta, is a twenty-eight-acre mixed-use community infill project on the former site of a polluting concrete plant. Designed by Victor

Dover and associates, Glenwood Park looked to the past for design elements of value that could be brought into the present to change the existing urban form, and succeeded in creating an intimate environment reminiscent of traditional neighborhoods from the turn of the century. Emphasizing quality and craftsmanship, they designed a mix of houses, townhouses and condominiums in historically appropriate architectural styles. The architects explained their aims: "Whereas conventional development emphasizes the private realm, auto dependency, single use pods, privacy, exclusivity, and bigger and bigger private houses Glenwood Park emphasizes the public realm, walkability, mixed uses, community, diversity, and quality over quantity."[5] Their design requires cars to travel slowly, emphasizing pedestrian comfort and safety. Parks incorporate storm water management systems that recharge groundwater. The commercial center has retail stores that serve the practical everyday needs of residents as well as being within walking distance of neighboring communities.

With the construction of these New Urbanist developments, local governments broke away from conventional ideas to help pave a way—perhaps I should say plant a way—into the future. The only challenge yet to be tackled by the New Urbanists is the inclusion of solar and other methods of energy production and the elimination of fossil fuel use onsite, the same challenge we all must face in our workplaces, homes and communities.

These efforts are laudable, but large-scale change cannot be left entirely to a handful of visionary planners and progressive politicians. We as consumers and citizens, especially at the local level, will play a crucial role in helping abate global warming and transitioning away from oil, natural gas and coal. As consumers, we can choose in every action to avoid the use of fossil fuels and select alternatives to products that rely on them for manufacturing and distribution. As citizens of our communities, we can fight for healthy living environments that fit our priorities and values. Many communities across the country have begun taking matters into their own hands to improve their relationship with the environment and revitalize their public spaces. They have also created arts councils and set money aside for projects like public murals and sculptures.

Many towns have passed building ordinances that address energy use, institute mandatory recycling programs, preserve adjacent agricultural lands through zoning, create farmers' markets and support locally owned businesses.

In his book *Deep Economy*, Bill McKibben advocates :

> The movement toward more local economies is the same direction we will have to travel to cope with the effects of these predicaments, not just to fend them off. The logic is fairly clear in a world threatened by ever-higher energy prices and even scarcer fossil fuel, you're better off in a relatively self-sufficient country or state or region. In a world increasingly rocked by wild and threatening weather, durable economies will be more useful than dynamic ones, and in both cases, the increased sense of community and heightened skill at democratic decision making that a more local economy implies will not simply increase our levels of satisfaction with our lives, but will also increase our chances of survival in a more dangerous world.[5]

So what specifically can and should we to do to make our home communities sustainable and desirable places to live in a post-fossil fuel world? Looking back to the 1800s at European towns and villages and even cities, which themselves consisted of groups of small villages, we see that each contained a center rich in activity. The center incorporated commerce, entertainment, the market and professional offices. It was also the seat of government. Citizens could reach any of these services or activities by means of an easy walk. Today we can redesign our towns and cities to create walkable villages that are characterized by their vibrancy and convenience. It cannot be emphasized enough that this is the most important step we can take to conserve energy and to live in harmony with nature. To accomplish this, jurisdictions will have to change zoning laws, redraw general plans and produce specific plans to redefine their suburbs as clusters of urban villages, as was done in Glenwood Park in Atlanta. We can begin the transition in our own city centers now by closing some streets to all but pedestrians and bicycles. Some cities have already accomplished this, closing shopping streets to automobiles and creating vibrant spaces with reduced noise and air pollution.

Where transportation is necessary, we will need to shift focus from the personal automobile to mass transit. Electric, hydrogen, and biofuel vehicles are much more expensive to own and operate than those that run on cheap fossil fuels; consequently, even accounting for more efficient designs, simple economics will force a decrease in car use. Instead, mass transit options such as electric buses and light rail can be used for commutes to urban centers and travel between communities, as in many European cities. For distance travel, we must rely less on airplanes—one of the most environmentally destructive modes of transportation—and use ships and high-speed trains.

The transportation of raw materials and finished goods around the world by supertankers is also destructive to our environment, so we will need to limit ourselves once again to local resources and cultivate local means of production. We need to support local small businesses and encourage the reemergence of local artisans and craftspeople to supply goods such as clothing, furniture, ceramics, and housewares. We also need to return to local food production, increasing the number of organic farmers marketing directly to local stores and consumers. The towns and villages we visited in this book were surrounded by some mix of agriculture and productive forests, adding both beauty to the scenery and security to the community. Through purchase or zoning, cities today can acquire and set aside lands for this purpose, some of which can be leased directly to farmers for organic food production. Cities can also restrict or limit the use of toxic chemicals within their jurisdictions.

We will need to create spaces for these farmers to sell directly to consumers as well. From early history, market day has been a rich tradition, one that offers the delightful experience of shopping in a festive atmosphere with music and other entertainment. In the early 1970s, the city of Davis authorized and began support for a farmers' market in its central park. The twice-weekly market has grown over the years, with a covered, open-air vending area added in 1994. Vendors sell organic foods, seasonal produce, eggs, cheese, fish, meats, poultry, nuts and grains. There are baked goods and ready-to-eat meals, clothing, jewelry, ceramics and artwork. In a vibrant atmosphere complete with music and activities for young children, shoppers are provided with all that is necessary to supply a healthy kitchen. The market is as much a social event as it is an opportunity to shop and support the local farmers and businesses. The adjoining park accommodates large groups for city-wide festivities. Spaces like these will be a key component of the revitalized communities of the future.

We can also improve our communities by making better use of land within existing super-sized suburban developments. Large backyards, for example, can be divided into private and public spaces for communal recreation, food production and socializing. A group of homeowners in Davis, California, ultimately named N Street Co-housing, did just this in the late 1970s, taking down backyard fences and creating a large commons. Participation was voluntary and everyone ultimately benefited from the creative design. The pattern was much like the Village Homes commons and resulted in more food production and social interaction between neighbors. Co-housing groups around the country have been building new projects in this style as well as redeveloping existing housing to create more communal, sustainable and friendly environments.

Energy production also needs to become a priority for municipalities. As new technologies allow greater decentralization of production, communities can create their own municipal energy companies to generate electricity from biofuels, wind, geothermal, or photovoltaic modules, whichever source or sources are most practical. They can require all new buildings to be powered by alternatives to fossil fuels, and in locales where sunlight is adequate; they can require solar water heating and photovoltaic electric generation.

Where atmospheric conditions do not present a health problem, wood can also be a local, renewable energy source. Historically, there have been times when careful management of forests has ensured a sustainable yield of wood products. The direct conversion of wood to heat is one of the most efficient sources of energy. Urban forests surrounding our towns and cities could be intermingled with agriculture, and, , could serve as a source of wood for direct heating in clean-burning stoves and fireplaces. Urban forests also serve as carbon sinks, helping to remove carbon dioxide from the atmosphere, as well as providing places for walking or quiet meditation.

Securing permanent water sources and adopting sustainable water conservation policies must be another priority in our communities. The use of natural drainages in the urban landscape will reduce water consumption even as it improves the aesthetic appeal of our towns and cities. The use of cisterns for collecting rainwater, a practice that has been used for centuries in many locations around the world, should become common practice.

To begin to restore the aesthetic qualities of our towns and cities, municipalities should hire or retain as consultants talented architects and landscape architects to oversee city projects and to advise homeowners and businesses. All too often important design decisions are made arbitrarily by people who lack proper training or talent, leaving behind an unsightly visual environment. Some American cities have maintained their beautiful environments through thoughtful regulation. The town center of Santa Barbara, California, and Aspen, Colorado, come to mind. While the wealth of these two cities has allowed residents to focus on such issues as preserving aesthetic appeal, places that would not be considered upscale, such as Ferndale, California and Grafton, Vermont have also managed to preserve their charm and visual appeal. With the political will, and under the supervision of talented architects or landscape architects, any town or city could begin a visual renaissance.

Although I have used the past in this book to provide inspiration for redesigning our communities, I do not mean to suggest that we should go back to the way we lived 150 years ago. In the future we will need to combine the best of the past and present, focusing on history's lessons as well as emerging ideas and technologies that promise to advance humanity and provide an environment capable of supporting a healthy population. In his 1973 book, *The Limits of the City*, Murray Bookchin expresses the idea powerfully:

> To restore urbanity as a meaningful terrain for socialization culture, and community, the megalopolis must be ruthlessly dissolved and replaced by new decentralized eco-communities, each carefully tailored to the natural ecosystem in which it is located. One might reasonably say that these eco-communities will possess the best features of the polis and medieval commune, supported by rounded eco-technologies

that rescale the most advanced elements of modern technology—including such energy sources as solar and wind power—to local dimensions. The equilibrium between town and country will be restored—not as a sprawling suburb that mistakes a lawn or patch of strategically placed trees for nature, but as an interactive functional eco-community that unites industry with agriculture, mental work with physical, individuality with community. Nature will not be reduced to a mere symbol of the natural, a spectatorial object to be seen from a window or during a stroll; it will become an integral part of all aspects of human experience, from work to play. Only in this form can the needs of nature become integrated with the needs of humanity and yield an authentic ecological consciousness that transcends the instrumentalist "environmental" outlook of the social and sanitary engineer.[6]

As we work to transform our lifestyles and architecture, bringing them into balance with nature, our success will depend on our ability to reeducate ourselves. Writers, scientists, economists, inventors and educators willing to intensify their efforts to explain the truth of the world today can be of immediate help, but we must also revolutionize the current educational system, making it more responsive to humanity's current plight. As it was with the Greeks and Romans and other successful societies, education is the foundation on which civilizations rest and the genesis for the form they take. Our educational system has been effective at producing specialists—teachers, researchers, professionals, clerical workers and laborers—to support the economic model that has been established by the corporate world. But this success has been paid for dearly, for we seem to have lost the broader perspective of the generalist or holistic thinkers who have an in-depth understanding of the interrelatedness of science, economics, politics and social and environmental problems.

We need an educational system that is more interdisciplinary, that prepares people for a world that is undergoing rapid change climatically, economically and socially. Our educational system needs to help produce individuals who are capable of understanding the current crises and who can help transform the world we live in today. Now more than ever, our educational system needs to nurture creativity, open-mindedness and tolerance. It must put more emphasis on the arts and personal creativity. It must explore philosophy, investigating principles of reality that transcend those of any particular science. Education must cover the full spectrum of science, emphasizing logic and critical thinking. Sherman Stein, in his book, *A Survival Guide for Outsiders*, lays out the critical thinking skills necessary to survive the complexities and distortions of the world today, pointing out how to avoid being easily manipulated by the self-serving propaganda of politicians, so-called experts and corporate pundits, providing the tools to defend ourselves in the midst of mass deception. Such a book should be required reading for every high school and college student, if not all of us.

We also need to devote more attention to practical or survival sciences which have not kept up with the complexities of the world today. From pre-historic times, people have depended on getting adequate lessons from their elders in order to survive . Education must now catch up. Daniel Goleman, in his 2009 book *Ecological Intelligence*, explains why humanity is struggling to survive in the industrialized world:

> Society has lost touch with what may be the singular sensibility crucial to our survival as a species. The routines of our daily lives go on completely disconnected from their adverse impacts on the world around us; our collective mind harbors blind spots that disconnect our everyday activities from the crises those same activities create in natural systems. Yet at the same time the global reach of our industry and commerce means that the impacts of how we live extend to the far corners of the planet. Our species threatens to consume and befoul the natural world at a rate that far exceeds our planet's carrying capacity. . .
>
> But nothing in our evolutionary past has shaped our brain for spotting palpable threats like the slow heating of the planet, neither the insidious spread of destructive chemical particulates into the air we breathe and things we eat, nor the inexorable destruction of vast swaths of flora and fauna on the planet. We can spot a menacing stranger's sinister face and immediately start walking in the other direction, but when it comes to global warming we shrug. Our brain excels in handling threats in the moment, but falters at managing those coming at us in some indefinite future.[7]

Goldman says the way out of this dilemma is to approach educa-tion from the point of view of ecological intelligence.

> "Ecological intelligence" [is] our ability to adapt to our ecological niche. Ecological refers to an understanding of or-ganisms and their ecosystems, and intelligence connotes the capacity to learn from experience and deal effectively with our environment. Ecological intelligence lets us apply what we learn about how human activity impinges on ecosystems so as to do less harm, and once again to live sustainably in our niche—these days, the entire planet.[8]

Additionally, we must include instruction in health, the envi-ronment and human impact on it, emergency response and global sustainability, and emphasize the interconnectedness of it all.

We also need to teach communication and group dynamics to help students learn to live in harmony with others. In *Unto This Last*, published in 1860, Ruskin advocated that the ideals of "gentleness and justice " be part of education. These principles need to be taught without naiveté, with the understanding that the world will always have to contend with selfishness, dishonesty, bullies and tyrants, and that we need strategies to deal with them.

Education for architects, landscape architects and urban plan-ners must likewise be based on an understanding of people's aesthet-ic and social needs and the environmental realities of the global life-support systems. Including in-depth exploration of philosophical thought in architectural training will broaden young practitioners' perspective and inspire their creativity. Standards for architects, landscape architects and urban planners must also be set higher, with a special designation for those who become fluent in the ability to create spaces and buildings with good proportion and meaningful and appropriate symbolism. We need architects, landscape archi-tects and planners who understand the true nature of their work in light of the unfolding realities of the twenty-first century and who are willing to produce environmentally transformational architec-ture. Just as the stones from obsolete or decaying buildings were re-cycled into the building of the Romanesque and Gothic houses, civic buildings, and cathedrals of the Middle Ages, enlightened artists of today must convert our aesthetically lacking and unsustainable urban conglomerations into places of beauty that can function in balance with nature. *In The Architecture of Happiness*, Alain de Botton describes how architects must be inspired to move beyond mediocrity and conventional thinking to produce work that embodies the deeper meaning of beauty found in the poetry of architecture:

> The places we call beautiful are. . . the work of those rare architects with the humility to interrogate themselves adequately about their desires and the tenacity to translate their fleeting apprehensions of joy into logical plans—a combination that enables them to create environments that satisfy needs we never consciously knew we even had.[9]

And now we must all interrogate ourselves as we watch what ultimately happens to a growth-oriented economy that is based on expanding consumerism and the pyramiding of wealth, as energy gets more expensive and resources more scarce. We must level with ourselves as members of the human race about our true needs. We can no longer wander helplessly with the frame of mind—a mental fog—created by our modern consumer-driven corporate culture. We need to escape its hypnotic spell into a state of mental clarity. We need to begin as soon as possible to transform our homes and buildings, transportation systems, industries, agriculture, towns and cities—all part of the substance of architecture—into sustainable and nurturing environments that we in our local communities take charge of.

We are fortunate today that we already have individuals, local governments, and national and global organizations actively working on the broad spectrum of environmental and social problems we face. Their work forms the foundation for what must become a great civil alliance to bring about a revolution in the way we live and work and, just as importantly, think. Social and economic change can be ours in the near future if we join these efforts. If we are willing to leave behind a world obsessed with the trappings of corporate consumerism, we can build a much more dynamic civilization that embraces the real prosperity found in our families and our communities, in our sense of beauty and creative potential, and in lives immersed in a harmonious relationship with nature.

APPENDIX

While political action to effect change is needed at the state, national, and international levels of government, we must remember that the greatest change, the change that we most desperately need, the change we can depend on, will come from what we ourselves do in the way we choose to live. The transportation we use, the products we buy and where and from whom we buy them, what we choose to eat, and how we convert our own homes and neighborhoods for energy and food production will have a direct effect on fossil carbon use and thus on our future. We must also work in our communities in ways that encourage local governments to function as they did in the past, when they controlled their own destinies as city-states and free towns. The following is a list of suggestions on how local governments can help us both survive climate change and bring back the poetry of architecture.

Recommendations for City-State Actions

- Redraw general plans and create specific plans for restructuring towns and cities to create clusters of urban villages. These plans should encourage a mix of uses so that daily needs are within walking distance.
- Provide transit options such as buses, light rail and trains connecting urban villages to each other as well as to major urban centers.
- Develop sustainable local municipal energy generation capacity.
- Develop sustainable local water systems.
- Secure enough local agricultural land through municipal ownership or zoning for sustainable, organic food production for the local population.
- Start the transition to alternative vehicles by closing some streets to all but bicycles and electric cars.
- Require electric photovoltaic generation on all new buildings where sunlight is adequate.
- Require solar water heating on all buildings where sunlight is adequate.
- Forbid the use of fossil fuels as an energy source in new buildings.
- Assist home and building owners in adding passive solar features for heating and cooling and encourage them to take the opportunity to increase the aesthetic value of their buildings by incorporating higher standards of design emphasizing personal and regional characteristics.
- Create an urban and peripheral forest program to serve as a carbon bank and for sustainable wood production for direct heating use.
- Adopt local standards for wood burning and stove fireplaces that take in to account atmospheric conditions and air quality.
- Start or strengthen local farmers' markets.
- Create programs to support small businesses that create goods and provide services locally.

- Set policies for recycling and waste reduction including composting of green material.
- Help homeowners and neighborhoods transform landscaping for food production and rainwater management and storage and in the process increase the aesthetic value of the landscape.
- Set up arts councils to improve community aesthetics and hold seminars and workshops to develop or refine a regional architectural character.
- Hire or retain architects and landscape architects to coordinate the design of town and city view-scapes.
- Foster and support organizations and groups working to make changes in design and lifestyle to meet the global environmental crisis, much like efforts to grow victory gardens during WWII.
- Lobby the federal government to levy a tax on fossil carbon fuels to offset the impact they have had on global warming. These revenues should be used for all levels of rail transportation and subsidies for the development of alternative power generation. Local governments should lobby for a portion of the tax as well, because their citizens will be the ones feeling the impacts of global warming.
- Encourage local school districts to include new curriculum that is based in the reality of the twenty-first century, with more emphasis on the areas mentioned in the previous chapter: personal health; communication and group dynamics; individuals' and society's collective impact on the environment; emergency response and survival strategies; and aid to the poor and needy. An additional set of courses should cover our artistic and creative nature and how it can be utilized to help us reach a higher level of self-actualization.

REFERENCES

<u>INTRODUCTION</u>

[1]Ellul, Jacques *The Betrayal of the West.* The Seabury Press, New York, 1978. [1]Adbusters. Sept./Oct. #85 Volume 17, Number 5

[2]There are several studies that give support to the claim that visual disharmony as a negative affect on mental health.

S. Galea, J. Ahern, S. Rudenstine, Z. Wallace, D. Vlahov. "Ur ban Built Environment and Depression" *Journal of Epidemi ology and Community Health* (October 2005)

S. Weich, Litwigg, G. Lewis. "Rural/Non-Rural differences in Rates of Common Mental Disorders in Britain." *The British Journal of Psychiatry* (Jan. 1 2006)

S. Weich, M. Blanchard, M. Prince, E. Burton. "Mental health and the Built Environment: Cross-sectional Survey of In dividual and Contextual Risk Factors for Depression" *British Journal of Psychiatry* (2002)

J. Maas, R. Verheiz, P. Groenewegen, S. de Vries, P. Spreeu wenberg. "Green Space, Urbanity and Health: How Strong is the Relation" *Journal of Epidemiology and Community Health*, 60: 587-592 doi: 10, 136/ jech 2005.043125. (2006)

[3]Intergovernmental Panel on Climate Change AR4 2007.

[4]Ibid

[5]Boissonade, P. *Life and Work in Medieval Europe.* Dover Publications, Inc., New York, 2002

[6]Klein, Richard G. *The Human Career: Human Biological and Cul tural Origins.* The University of Chicago Press, Chi cago, 2009. Prentice Hall, New Jersey, 2008.

[7] Fagan, Brian M. *World Prehistory: A Brief Introduction.* Pear son/Prentice Hall, New Jersey, 2008.

[8]Jobling, M.A, Hurles, M.E., Tyler-Smith, C. *Human Evolution ary Genetics: Origins, Peoples & Disease.* Garland Science, New York, 2004.

[9]Ruskin, John, *The Poetry of Architecture.* George Routledge and Sons, London, 1907.

[10]Diamond, Jared, *Collapse: How Societies Choose to Fail or Succeed*, Penguin Group, New York, 2005.

[11] Fischer ,Louis, (Edited by)*The Essential Gandhi, an Anthology of his Writings on his Life, Work and Ideas.* . Vintage Books, New York, 1962.

CHAPTER I

[1]De Botton, Alain, *The Architecture of Happiness.* Pantheon Books, New York, 2006.

[2]There are several studies that give support to the claim that visual disharmony as a negative affect on mental health.

S. Galea, J. Ahern, S. Rudenstine, Z. Wallace, D. Vlahov. "Urban Built Environment and Depression" *Journal of Epidemiology and Community Health* (October 2005)

S. Weich, Litwigg, G. Lewis. "Rural/Non-Rural differences in Rates of Common Mental Disorders in Britain." *The British Journal of Psychiatry* (Jan. 1 2006)

S. Weich, M. Blanchard, M. Prince, E. Burton. "Mental health and the Built Environment: Cross-sectional Survey of Individual and Contextual Risk Factors for Depression" *British Journal of Psychiatry* (2002)

J. Maas, R. Verheiz, P. Groenewegen, S. de Vries, P. Spreeuwenberg. "Green Space, Urbanity and Health: How Strong is the Relation" *Journal of Epidemiology and Community Health*, 60: 587-592 doi: 10, 136/ jech 2005.043125. (2006)

[3]Ruskin, John, *The Seven Lamps of Architecture, Virtue & Company Ltd.* London, 1907.

[4]Dubos, Rene, *Beast or Angel: Choices that Make Us Human.* New York Charles Scribner's Sons, 1974.

[5]Ruskin, John *The Stones of Venice,* Da Capo, Cambrigde, MA, 2003.

[6]Kemp, Wolfgang, *The Desire of My Eyes: The Life and Work of John Ruskin,* The Noonday Press, New York, 1990.

[7]Ibid

[8]Pinker, Steven, *The Blank Slate,* Penguin Group. New York, 2002.

[9]Ibid

[10]Ibid

[11]Ruskin, John, *The Poetry of Architecture*. George Routledge and Sons, London, 1907.

[12]Ruskin, John, *The Seven Lamps of Architecture*, Virtue & Company Ltd. London, 1907.

[13]Pinker, Steven, *The Blank Slate*, Penguin Group. New York, 2002.

CHAPTER II

[1]Fagan, Brian M. *The Great Warming. Climate Change and The Rise and Fall of Civilizations*. Bloomsbury Press, New York, 2008.

[2]Fagan, Brian M. *World Prehistory: A Brief Introduction*. Pearson/ Prentice Hall, New Jersey, 2008.

[3]Ibid

[4]Mithen, Steven, *After the Ice: A global human history 20,000- 50,000   BC*, Harvard University Press, 2003.

[5]Ibid

[6]Ibid

[7]Cunliffe, Barry *Europe Between The Oceans*. Yale University Press, 2008

[8]Ibid

[9]Ibid

[10]Ibid

[11]Wilson, Peter J. *The Domestication of the Human Species*. Yale University Press, 1991

[12]Ibid

[13]Cunliffe, Barry *Europe Between The Oceans*. Yale Univer sity Press, 2008

[14]Wilson, Peter J. *The Domestication of the Human Species*. Yale University Press, 1991

[15]Mohen, Jean-Pierre, Christiane Eluère, *The Bronze Age in Europe: gods, heroes and treasures*. Thames and Hudson Ltd, London 2000

[16]Ibid

[17]Powell, T.G.E. *The Celts.* Thames & Hudson, 1983

[18]Ibid

[19]Davis, Courtney, *Celtic Ornamentation: The Art of the Scribe,* Blandford Press, 1996.

[20]Powell, T.G.E. *The Celts.* Thames & Hudson, 1983

[21]Ibid

[22]Plato, *The Republic,* Penguin Books, 2003

[23]Cunliffe, Barry *Europe Between The Oceans.* Yale University Press, 2008

[24]Ibid

[25]Ludwig, Emil, *The Mediterranean.* Whittlesey House, New York, 1942

[26]Fletcher, Sir Banister, *A History of Architecture: On The Comparative Method, Seventeenth Edition.* Charles Scribner's Son, New York, 1961

[27]Boissonade, P. *Life and Work in Medieval Europe.* Dover Publications, Inc., New York, 2002

[28]Ibid

[29]Ibid

[30]Fletcher, Sir Banister, *A History of Architecture: On The Comparative Method, Seventeenth Edition.* Charles Scribner's Son, New York, 1961

[31]Boissonade, P. *Life and Work in Medieval Europe.* Dover Publications, Inc., New York, 2002

[32]Ibid

[33]Ibid

[34]Fletcher, Sir Banister, *A History of Architecture: On The Comparative Method, Seventeenth Edition.* Charles Scribner's Son, New York, 1961

[35]Boissonade, P. *Life and Work in Medieval Europe.* Dover Publications, Inc., New York, 2002

[36]Ibid

[37]Powell, T.G.E. *The Celts.* Thames & Hudson, 1983

[38]Fletcher, Sir Banister, *A History of Architecture: On The Comparative Method, Seventeenth Edition.* Charles Scribner's Son, New York, 1961

[39]Boissonade, P. *Life and Work in Medieval Europe.* Dover Publications, Inc., New York, 2002

[40]Ibid

[41]Ibid

[42]Ibid

[43]Ibid

[44]Ibid

[45]Ibid

[46]Ibid

[47]Lewis, Mumford, *Techniques & Civilization.* Harcourt Brace & Company, 1934.

[48]Boissonade, P. *Life and Work in Medieval Europe.* Dover Publications, Inc., New York, 2002

[49]Ibid

[50]Stefanon, Laurence, Antoine Rego, Michael Renaud, *A Brief History of the Hundred Years' War 1337-1453,* Collection Breve Histoire.

[51]Boissonade, P. *Life and Work in Medieval Europe.* Dover Publications, Inc., New York, 2002

[52]Fletcher, Sir Banister, *A History of Architecture: On The Comparative Method, Seventeenth Edition.* Charles Scribner's Son, New York, 1961

[53]Shorto, Russell, *Descartes' Bones: A Skeletal History of the Conflict Between Faith and Reason.* Doubleday, 2008.

[54]Ibid

[55]Ibid

[56]Ibid

[57]Kemp, Wolfgang, *The Desire of My Eyes: The Life Work of John Ruskin,* Noonday, 1983.

[58]Harvie, Christopher & H.C.G. Matthew, *Nineteenth-Century Britain, Oxford University Press,* Oxford, 2000.

[59]Ibid

[60]Ibid

[61]Ibid

[62]Warmington, Allan, *Campden: A New History.* CADHAS, Chip ping Campden, 2005.

[63]Ibid

[64]Ibid.

[65]Ebenezer Howard, *Garden Cities of Tomorrow.* MIT Press, Cambridge, Mass., 1965

CHAPTER IV

[1]Strayer, Joseph R. *On the Medieval Origins of the Modern State.* Princeton University Press, 2005

[2] Dalton,G., *Aristotle Discovers the Economy in Primitive, Archaic and Modern Economies: Essays of Karl Polanyi* ed. , Boston 1971, 78-115

[3]Hayes, Denis "A Plan for the Solar Revolution," *Solar Today,* April/May 2009.

[4]Brown, Lester, *Plan B 3.0, Mobilizing to Save Civilization.* W.W. Norton and Co., New York, 2008.

[5]McKibben, Bill ,*Deep Economy: The Wealth of Communities and the Durable Future,* Times Books, 2007.

[6]Bookchin, Murray, *The Limits of the City,* Harper & Row, New York, 1974.

[7]Goleman, Daniel, *Ecological Intelligence,* Doubleday, New York, 2009.

[8]Goleman, Daniel, *Ecological Intelligence,* Doubleday, New York, 2009.

[9]De Botton, Alain *The Architecture of Happiness.* Pantheon Books, New York, 2006.

General References

Bailey, Brian, *The English Village Green*. Robert Hale, London, 1985.

Boissonade, P. *Life and Work in Medieval Europe*. Dover Publications, Inc., New York, 2002.

Corbett, Michael, *A Better Place to Live*. Rodale, Pennsylvania, 1981.

Cunliffe, Barry *Europe Between The Oceans*. Yale University Press, 2008

Davis, Courtney, *Celtic Ornamentation: The Art of the Scribe*, Blandford Press, 1996.

Descartes, Rene, Laurence J. Lafleur (trans.) (1960). *Discourse on Method and Meditations*. New York: The Liberal Arts Press.

De Botton, Alain, *The Architecture of Happiness*. Pantheon Books, New York, 2006.

Dubos, Rene, *Beast or Angel: Choices that Make Us Human*. (New York Charles Scribner's Sons, 1974)

Ellul, Jacques *The Betrayal of the West*. The Seabury Press, New York, 1978.

Fagan, Brian M. *The Great Warming. Climate Change and The Rise and Fall of Civilizations*. Bloomsbury Press, New York, 2008.

Fagan, Brian M. *World Prehistory: A Brief Introduction*. Pearson/ Prentice Hall, New Jersey, 2008.

Fischer , Louis, (Edited by) *The Essential Gandhi, an Anthology of his Writings on his Life, Work and Ideas*. Vintage Books, New York, 1962.

Fletcher, Sir Banister, *A History of Architecture: On The Comparative Method, Seventeenth Edition*. Charles Scribner's Son, New York, 1961.

Gore, Al, *An Inconvenient Truth*, Rodale, New York, 2006.

Hall, Stephen S., *"Iceman Mystery" National Geographic*. July 2007:

Howard, Ebenezer, *Garden Cities of Tomorrow*. MIT Press,

Cambridge, Mass., 1965

Kemp, Wolfgang, *The Desire of My Eyes: The Life Work of John Ruskin*, Noonday, 1983.

Lewis, Mumford, *Techniques & Civilization*. Harcourt Brace & Company, 1934.

Mohen, Jean-Pierre, Christiane Eluère, *The Bronze Age in Europe: gods, heroes and treasures*. Thames and Hudson Ltd, London 2000

McKay, Alexander G., *Houses, Villas, and Palaces in the Roman World*. Thames and Hudson, London, 1975

Mithen, Steven, *After the Ice: A global human history 20,000-50,000 BC*, Harvard University Press, 2003.

Pinker, Steven, *The Blank Slate*, Penguin Group. New York, 2002.

Plato, *The Republic*, Penguin Books

Powell, T.G.E. *The Celts*. Thames & Hudson, 1983.

Price, T. Douglas, James A. Brown, *Prehistoric hunter-gatherers: the emergence of cultural complexity*, Academic Press, 1985

Ruskin, John, *The Poetry of Architecture*. George Routledge and Sons, London, 1907.

Stefanon, Laurence, Antoine Rego, Michael Renaud, *A Brief History of the Hundred Years' War 1337-1453*, Collection Breve Histoire

Shorto, Russell, *Descartes' Bones: A Skeletal History of the Conflict Between Faith and Reason*. Doubleday, 2008.

Strayer, Joseph R. *On the Medieval Origins of the Modern State*. Princeton University Press, 2005

Wilson, Paul J. *The Domestication of the Human Species*. Yale University Press, 1991

Warmington, Allan, *Campden: A New History*. CADHAS, Chipping Campden, 2005.

Town and Village References

<u>Dinan</u>

"Dinan Pays de Rance: Discovery Tours town of Art and History", Office de Tourisme Dinan

"Pays touristique de Dinan: #4 Season / 2006-2007", Le Pays Touristique de Dian

<u>Domme:</u>

Bentley, James, *Fort Towns of France: The Bastides of the Dordogne & Aquitaine.* Tauris Parke Books, London, 1993

Bentley, James, Hugh Palmer, *The Most Beautiful Villages of the Dordogne.* Thames and Hudson Ltd., New York, 1996.

Pungnere, Maurice, *Domme en Perigord: Historie de la ville et du chateau.* Le Livre d'histoire-Lorisse, Paris, 2004.

<u>Monpazier:</u>

Bentley, James, *Fort Towns of France: The Bastides of the Dordogne & Aquitaine.* Tauris Parke Books, London, 1993.

Bentley, James, Hugh Palmer, *The Most Beautiful Villages of the Dordogne.* Thames and Hudson Ltd., New York, 1996.

"Plan Bastide De Monpazier et de Son Caton," Office de Tourisme Du Monpazierois

<u>Sare:</u>

"Le Musee Basque & de l'histoire de Bayonne. Euskal Museoa"

"Ortillopitz: La Maison Baswue de Sare 1660," Pays Basque – Cote Basque 2006.

Jobling, M.A., Hurles, M. E., Tyler-Smith, C., *Human Evolutionary Genetics: Origins, Peoples & Disease,* Garland Publishing, 2004.

ALTIMIRA CAVE AND SANTILLANA DEL MAR:

Campuzano Enrique, Lasheras, Jose A., *Santillana and Alta mira*. Editorial Everest, 1998.

Museo de Altamira

ARCOS:

Regordan, Perez M., *From Arcos to Ronda Around the Gad itans Highlands*, The White Towns Route, 2005

"Arcos," Local Government Tourist Office

"Archaeological Museum of Granada," Museos De Andalucia

"Andalucia, Granada" Junta de Andalucia Consejeria de Tur ismo, Comercio y Deporte

ALHAMBRA AND GRANADA:

Gallego y Burin, Antonio, *Granada: An Artistic and Histori cal Guide to the City*. Editorial Comares, Granada, 1992.

Irving, Washington, *Tales of the Alhambra*. Ediciones Miguel Sanchez, Madrid 1994

"The Alhambra and Generalife," Patronato de la Alhambra y Generalife, Editorial Comares, Spain, 1999.

Archaeological Museum of Granada - Museos de Andalucia

VERS:

The Pont Du Gard: and the Roman Aqueduct from Uzes to Nimes. Casa Editrice Bonechi, 2003

IN SEARCH OF THE ROMANS:

Napoli, Electa, *Pompeii: Guide to the Site.* Ministero per i Beni e le Attivita Culturali Soprintendenza Archeologica di Pompei, Italy, 1998.

Garcia y Garcia, Laurentino, *Pupils, Teachers and Schools in Pompeii: Childhood, Youth and Culture in the Roman Era.* Bardi Editore, Rome, 2005

CORTONA:

   Holder, Philancy N., *Cortona in Context: The History and Ar*
      chitecture of an Italian Hill Town to the 17th Century.
      Arti Tipografiche Toscane, Tuscany, 1999.
   MAEC: Museo dell' Accademia Etrusca e della Citta di Cor
      tona

ASSISI:

   Della Porta, P.M, Guide to Assisi: History and Art. Editrice
      Minerva, Assisi 2001
   Roman Forum and Archaeological Collection
   The Basilica of St Francis and the Sacro Convento
   Temple of Minerva
   Guida di Assisi, Maps

RADOVLJICA:

   "Questions about Slovenia" Zalozba Turista, Kranj, 2003.
   Vodnikov, Zbirka, Radovljica. Kulturni In Naravni Spome
      niki Slovenije.
   The Municipial Museum of Radovljica
   The Museum of Apiculture
   The Sivec House

KASTLERUTH:

   South Tyrol Museum of Archeology

HALLSTATT:

   Cultural Heritage Museum
   Hall, Stephen S., *"Iceman Mystery" National Geographic.* July
      2007:
   Jarosch, Lipp, Lammerhuber, *Hallstatt-Dachstein-Salz*
      kammergut, Icoomos.

EGER:

   Hungarian History in a Nutshell, Merhavia.
   Istvan Dobo Castle Museum

CESKY/KRUMLOV:
Cesky Krumlov Museum of Architecture and Craft
Pavelec, Petr, Ckesky Krumlov: an enchanting town in the
    heart of Europe. Petr Pavelec, Ceske Budejovice, 2000.

ROTHENBURG:
Rothenburg on the Tauber. Kunstverlad Edm. von Konig
    GmbH & Co. KG, Heidelberg/Dielheim, 2000
Rothenburg Map & Guide, Rothenburg Tourismus Service
The Imperial City Museum
CHIPPING CAMPDEN:
Warmington, Allan, Campden: A New History. CADHAS,
    Chipping Campden, 2005
Blockley Church, "Twelve Centuries of Worship & Witness,
    Church History Exhibition" Jeremy Bourne, May 2006
Sandry, Claire, Chipping Campden: Town Trail. The Camp
    den Society

HAWKSHEAD:
Canning, Paul, Historic Lakeland. Ian Allan Ltd., London,
    1989.
Walker, Freda M. "A Little History and Guide to Hawks
    head"   Reed's Limited.
Brantwood: John Ruskin's home 1872-1900
Musemum of Lakeland Life: 2006
Welcome to Stonehenge: World Heritage Site

Photo Credits

ALL PHOTOS TAKEN BY MICHAEL CORBETT, EXCEPTIONS IN ITALICS.

CHAPTER 1:
Page 16.....Coniston Hall, *Drawing by John Ruskin*
Page 32.....19th Century European Painting, *Unknown Artist*

CHAPTER 2:
Page 38.....Painted Images – Altamira Cave, Spain, *National Museum and Research Centre of Altamira*
Page 42.....Stonehenge
Page 44.....Medieval Carcassonne
Page 46.....Lion Gate, *Drawing by Michael McDermott*
Page 48.....Grave Marker
Page 60.....Collegiate Church of Santillana Del Mar
Page 64.....Notre Dame
Page 65.....1380 Gothic Residence – Chipping Campden

CHAPTER 3
Page 78.....Partial Map of Europe 2006, *Michael McDermott*
Page 80.....Dinan
Page 82.....Stone Wall
Page 83.....Town Gate
Page 84.....Early Morning Rooftops
Page 87.....Saint-Sauveur Basilica
Page 88.....Half-Timbered House
Page 89.....Renaissance Style House
Page 90.....Chateau Near Brittany Boarder
Page 92.....Domme
Page 94.....To the Valley Floor
Page 95.....Stone Carved Windows Casements
Page 95.....Dormer Windows
Page 96.....Market Building, *Steve Tracy*
Page 98.....Main Street

ACKNOWLEDGEMENTS

There are many people whom I would like to thank for helping me craft my words into a form that honors the ideas and passion behind them. First, I would like to acknowledge my closest friend and partner, Elizabeth McDermott, for helping conceptualize this book and fill in pertinent details, ideas, and points of discussion where they were missing or vague. Her assistance on the journey, making observations and gathering information, went far beyond what is represented in the text.

Digitally altering the photographs so that they would more closely re-create the scenes as Ruskin might have experienced them 150 years ago required computer expertise exceeding my capabilities and patience. Michael J McDermott, took on the task with considerable talent and perseverance, clearing signs, wires, inappropriately dressed people and automobiles from the photographs, and then rebuilding any architecture that was altered during the transformation. In addition, Michael formatted the book with Adobe InDesign and provided a well-rendered drawing of the Lion Gate, which I was unable to photograph. In the end Michael was involved in the editing and actually produced the book cover to cover. I thank him for his hard work and patience.

I would like to thank Binuta Sudhakaran for her help both in reviewing the content and assisting in the formatting of the final draft at that critical time before production. I would also like to thank my friend Steve Tracy, who provided several photos of the Bastide Montpazier, introduced me to the special nature of the bastides, and offered helpful comments on early drafts. I appreciate very much my time spent with Martin Barnes and his insights from living in Vers, a village that dates back to Roman times.

Special thanks go to the highly talented Italian photographer Giancarlo Giupponi, who shared with me his photograph of Assisi. Also, thanks to photographer Tom Deninger, for his help in architectural photography, digital camera use, and Photoshop. I deeply appreciate those who provided editorial assistance. Dan Sullivan, Janice Barrow, Jean Walraven, Mimi Kusch and especially Julian Foley — all helped me make the book readable. Mark Hoyer played an extremely important role in editorial assistance from the first go-around to the final touches. Thanks to Jonathan Terre for his positive support and synopsis for the back cover.

Anthropologist Luke Barton offered his expertise on European pre-history. John Malcolm, Professor (Emeritus) of Philosophy at UC Davis, offered many helpful insights and comments on ancient philosophy. Historian Mel Draper reviewed the manuscript and assisted in checking the accuracy of historic events. Robert and Barbara Summer helped with the final review of this book. Robert Summer, the father of environmental psychology has been a mentor since I first read his book *A Personal Space*. Sherman Stien, the author of *A Survival Guide for Outsiders*, also helped with the final review and insight on publishing.

I appreciate also those who read early drafts and made comments: Dennis Dingemans, John and Lynn Lofland, Eve Westbessier, Stacey and Lucas Frerichs, David Thompson, Kelly Van Boxtel, Terry Bisson,David Robertson, and my son Christopher Corbett and his wife Nicole Brashear, who also joined me on a leg of the journey, offering their insights. Tara McDermott was also of considerable help doing initial research and assisting in conceptualizing the writing. I deeply appreciate the efforts of Janet Gift of The Secretariat who translated my scribbles into legible words, even from scanned e-mails sent all the way from Europe and provided editorial assistance throughout the process. I also very much appreciate Rick Steve's *Europe Through the Back Door* publications, which helped me find appropriate lodging and provided accurate written vignettes of many of the places I visited. I was also fortunate to have numerous books and articles to draw from. I made considerable use of Life and Work in Medieval Europe by P. Boissonnade and Europe Between the Oceans 9000 BC-AD 1000 by Barry Cunliffe. Just as I was completing the manuscript, I came across a newly published book, *The Blank Slate*, by Steven Pinker, which was helpful in supporting several of my arguments. I believe it is a must read for architects, artists and social scientists.

To all, I offer my heart-felt thanks.
Michael N. Corbett

INDEX